WHEN YOU HAVEN'T
GOT A PRAYER

This book is about prayer, the quest of the soul for God. But running through it like a leit motif is the love and grace of God and his search to be known and loved by us. In fact, as Stuart Sacks makes abundantly plain, it is his love for us that makes our communion with Him possible. Is prayer a problem for you? It must be, because it is for everyone. But I say, Take time to read this book; you'll profit from it. And after that take time to pray! It is the noblest activity in which any of us can ever be engaged.

James Montgomery Boice
Tenth Presbyterian Church, Philadelphia, USA

Stuart Sacks has given an honest account of his struggle when he hadn't got a prayer to offer in times when faith is tested and almost lost. In such times, life crowds out the desire to seek God and personal anxieties crush the soul.

Like most of us in the discipline of prayer, he is struggling to develop a rich and satisfying communion with God, because, as he says, 'our communion with God will inevitably be determined by our conception of Him'.

Stuart encourages us to recognise God as the God of grace alone. Then, 'prayer rightly becomes our response to His undeserved favour'.

Jessie MacFarlane,
Co-ordinator, Telephone Prayer Chain Ministry, Great Britain

WHEN YOU HAVEN'T GOT A PRAYER

Help for Those Struggling to Pray

Stuart D. Sacks, Th.D.

Christian Focus Publications

© 1994 Stuart Sacks
ISBN 1-85792-092-9

Published by
Christian Focus Publications Ltd
Geanies House, Fearn, Ross-shire,
IV20 1TW, Scotland, Great Britain.

Cover design by Donna Macleod

AMERICAN MISSIONARY FELLOWSHIP
Box 368 - 672 Conestoga Rd
Villanova, PA 19085
Tel. (215) 527-4439 FAX (215) 527-4720

Printed and bound in Great Britain by
The Guernsey Press Co. Ltd, Guernsey, Channel Islands

Contents

A Word About the Author:

Before becoming Advisor for Continuing Education with The American Missionary Fellowship, Villanova, Pennsylvania, Stuart Sacks was a Presbyterian pastor for eighteen years. Before earning a Doctorate in Old Testament (Southwest Theological Seminary) his career in music included the composition of a commissioned work for the C.B.S. Television Network.

A Word About the Contents:

Do you find it difficult to pray? Does it seem like an insurmountable task to enjoy the presence of God? Have bitter experiences made your devotional life all but non-existent? You're not alone. The author, too, personally struggles to realise a meaningful prayer life. Through Biblically supported personal experience he offers encouragement and direction for you when it seems you haven't got a prayer.

for
Sharon

Love never fails...
(1 Corinthians 13:8)

FOREWORD

Recently, the controversial Roman Catholic theologian, Hans Kung, published a brief monograph on another controversial person, Wolfgang Amadeus Mozart. Kung sought to probe whatever hint of vestigial Catholicism could be found in the erratic rebel son-of-the-church, Mozart. He scanned beyond the horizon of Mozart's comic-tragic personal life and through the scurrilous Hollywood caricature of 'Amadeus'. He finds a yearning for 'transcendence' in the delicate, at times moody music of Mozart.

Of Mozart one thing is sure. His prodigious music points the listener heavenward by the sheer majesty of its scope - with or without the composer's intent.

In this book there is no need to guess about the author's intent. Stuart Sacks is a theologian. He is also a musician of the highest order. I have listened to his musical compositions and arrangements and have experienced through them the rising of my soul in exaltation before the beauty of the holiness of God.

There is an unbreakable link between the Holy and the Beautiful. The link is so solid that the artist who burns in hostility toward God cannot help but bear witness to God when he produces something beautiful. The beauty screams louder than the vice of the artist. Like Balaam, the unbelieving artist blesses God in spite of himself.

When Dr. Sacks blesses God in his music and writing he is not doing it in spite of himself. He sees the link between the

Holy and the Beautiful. He loves the link between the Holy and the Beautiful.

I am a frustrated amateur musician. My fingers are wild and undisciplined. My ear is alloyed with tin. My rhythm is left in the metronomes. I have difficulty with the language of music. It is a hermeneutical problem, a problem of translation. Notes written in ink upon a page comprise a most difficult language for me. Somehow for the beauty to happen those notes have to be transformed into music.

Dr. Sacks has no such trouble with the language of music. He understands it. He can translate it. The notes cease being notes and become music at his touch.

But what does this have to do with prayer? As I read this book I heard music. There is a lyrical quality to his prose. His prose, at times a tortuous quest for the presence of God, faces the dissonance of life and yet finds a marvellous harmonic resolution. The book reveals a man who has spent a lifetime in the tension of delayed resolution who finds his rest in God.

Reading this book is a bit like eavesdropping on a soul naked before God. The panting heart is laid bare. There is an unmistakable classical quality to it in that in the author's pursuit of prayer we feel, almost in a tactile way, the ghosts of great spiritual warriors of history, who have held Sacks in their grip. Dr. Sacks' Jewish background comes through. He reveals himself as a true Bar Mitzvah, a 'son of the commandment'.

His soul merges with the spirit of Abraham who found God in the Stygian darkness of the night, of Moses who met with God amid the dreadful smoke and thunder of Sinai, of David who kept his pillow wet with his tears, of Paul whose prayers were without ceasing, and of the saints of church history who would settle for nothing less than God Himself.

This book is about the soul's quest for God. It is not an abstract treatise interested in expressions about God. It is not a primer on spiritual magic. It is a map for the serious seeker of the living God, for the person who aches for God Himself.

This may not be Stuart Sacks' first symphony ... but it is surely his best.

R. C. Sproul
Orlando, 1993

Author's Prefatory Note

I've just finished teaching a brief course on composition at a nearby university. Part of our class time was devoted to the study of the great Passacaglia in C minor by J. S. Bach, one of musical literature's most outstanding works. While this book has only a little bit to do with music —and certainly makes no pretence at greatness—it has something in common with a passacaglia. That musical discipline is characterized by the repetition of a melodic theme, a recognizable line in the bass which runs the length of the piece. Sometimes the motif has so many other elements working around it that you almost forget its presence; yet sooner or later the listener is again made aware of that distinct unifying element.

My apologies to those gifted authors and speakers whose work I have failed to acknowledge, yet it is interwoven with my own. Their thoughts doubtless framed part of my somewhat sketchy sermon notes from which parts of my manuscript were drawn. My personal thanks to Colin Morison of Christian Focus Publications and to Dr. Duane Bartruff of the American Missionary Fellowship without whose encouragement this book would not have been written.

In this work, all its diverse elements are bound together by the central theme of God's grace: His love for us, sovereignly and undeservedly lavished upon us in Jesus Christ. The reader will observe this recurrent feature for it prominently fills these pages. Although I've reached the age where it's possible to repeat myself unintentionally, I hope the reader will be refreshed by phrases which may strike him as being somewhat repetitive; for without grace there can be no meaningful prayer. If we hope to have a prayer we must begin by magnifying the God of grace. This I have tried to do — *Soli Deo Gloria*.

WHEN
YOU
HAVEN'T
GOT
A
PRAYER

'It is as important to remind as it is to inform.'
Samuel Johnson

1
Embracing Reality

Hardly anything tells us as much about our Christian vitality as does our prayer life. It is at once the most noble and necessary of Christian exercises; it is also the hardest. Ministers often find it as difficult as do the flock entrusted to their care. Sadly, we are plagued by a lack of self-discipline not to mention an often woefully inadequate concept of the scope and purpose of prayer. In 1952, a Ph.D. candidate at Princeton asked the distinguished visitor, Albert Einstein, a question which has become even more commonplace among doctoral students: 'What is there left to write upon?' The learned scientist responded: 'Find out about prayer; someone must find out about prayer!' Despite our acknowledgement of the inestimable worth of prayer we often find it perplexing and make short shrift of it again and again. The Puritan, Thomas Watson, lamented, 'Christ went more readily to the cross than we do to the throne of grace.

Chief among the reasons for prayer is the extraordinary fellowship to which God has called us (1 Corinthians 1:9). Jesus often separated Himself from His disciples to spend evenings savouring uninterrupted communion with His heavenly Father. It was by way of that intimate fellowship that

He was able to tell His disciples, 'I have food to eat that you know nothing about' (John 4:32). I want to eat that food. My desire is for prayer to become a vital, overarching power in my life.

Yet spending time alone with God has often been a Herculean task. C. S. Lewis understood well the difficulties involved: 'The moment you wake up each morning, all your wishes and hopes for each day rush at you like wild animals. And the first job each morning consists in shoving it all back; in listening to that other voice, taking that other point of view, letting that other, larger, stronger, quieter life come flowing in.'

I confess at the outset that my prayer life has been less than it should be—that I have often neglected it in favour of many pressing, more 'practical' things. Regrettably I have frequently allowed my emotions to control my prayer life, dictating its lamentably limited dimensions. I am struggling to develop a rich and satisfying communion with God; it is not yet something I possess. But out of my ongoing struggles I've come to recognize certain truths—realities which have helped me in my quest. I offer them to you with the hope that you will find them beneficial and encouraging.

FALSE START
It was the Sabbath. I sat in assembly with a hundred other squirming children at Beth Emeth Synagogue. Our rabbi ascended his platform, looked at us with a pained expression, and uttered these words: 'There are some of you who do not believe in God.' I could not have been more than ten years of age at the time yet the event is still fresh in my mind. I recall thinking, 'How is it possible that what the rabbi says is so? How can a Jew *not* believe in God? We are His chosen people.'

Notwithstanding, the belief nurtured by my synagogue—its

name meant 'House of Truth'—only served up part of the truth: an inadequate diet with scant portions of holy righteousness and judgment. As a result I thought that my failure to live up to the Law's demands was not a severe problem that needed somehow to be dealt with and overcome. What I did realise, however, was a growing sense of God's distance from me; and I felt as though that distance could never be bridged.

If I had been living a few thousand years earlier my worship experience would have been significantly different. At the appointed time I would have brought a perfect male animal to the entrance of the tent of meeting where I would have laid my hand on the sacrificial victim's head and, before killing it on the north side of the altar, tell the priest why I was bringing the burnt offering. I would have listened gladly to the priest's response, declaring my offering acceptable, whereupon I would have watched the priests collect the blood as it poured out from the dying animal and witnessed their splashing it against the sides of the altar. Then I would have dismembered the victim and beheld the drama of the priest placing its parts upon the altar as its relentless fires consumed my burnt offering. I would have sensed that my relationship with Yahweh—my access to Him—was profoundly affected by this prescribed Biblical ritual (cf. Leviticus 1).

But that was then. Now there remained no cleansing ritual, no sacrificial soothing aroma; only a contrived vestige of what we Jews called *Ha Yom*, The Day (of Atonement). According to our rabbis it was on *Ha Yom* that Moses descended for a second time from Sinai, not only with new tablets of the law but also with reassuring words of God's forgiveness for my people's transgressions (cf. Exodus 34: 29-32). Moses and the priests were our great mediators then; now my people resorted to methods of their own—ways without regard for any mediator, human or divine.

On one high holy day my father and I arrived late for the synagogue's worship service. We found the sanctuary full to overflowing; in fact, there wasn't even standing room. A disconcerted father looked at his teenage son and said, 'Well, Stuart, God knows we made an effort to be here; that's what matters.' But did it? How could I be assured that our efforts to attend the service made our prayers—made us—acceptable to the One whom we reverently called *Adonai* ('Lord')?

For me there was an undeniable sense of futility in all religious exercises, for none of them enabled me to enter beyond the curtain where the Holy One of Israel dwelt, remote and inaccessible. Many years would pass before my soul recognized the Eternal Priest who brought His own blood into the most holy place, rending its curtain on my behalf (Hebrews 6:19-20), thereby bringing me into fellowship with Him. How God traversed sin's barrier in His Christ became the basis for everything truly joyful for me ever since my life's watershed experience: simple trust in all that the Lord Jesus accomplished for me on the cross.

What has been identified by poets as the explosive power of this new affection made my early devotional life full as I 'delighted in the richest of fare' (Isaiah 55:2). Several years passed before I noticed that a certain leanness had crept in. What was once a delight had become little more than a duty; times of deep communion with God were becoming more and more attenuated. Personal problems (both emotional and physical) only added to my spiritual dilemma for it seemed as if the heavens were impenetrable to my numerous petitions for wholeness.

REFRESHMENT FROM THE ROOTS

My thinking about God needed to rest more squarely upon His authoritative word and less upon unreliable traditions and the fickle suggestions of conscience. The Judaism of my youth had emphasized the importance of doing what the Torah said. According to our rabbis, acceptance by God was based upon a mixture of dogged effort and divine mercy. Each year the high holy days were seen as an opportunity for His mercy to catch up with and compensate for our failure to satisfactorily obey Yahweh's commandments.

Yet our rabbi's annual intonation that our sins were forgiven did not carry the same weight as the word of Yahweh which said He would not leave the guilty unpunished (Exodus 34:7); the soul that sinned would die (Ezekiel 18:4). Moreover, the Almighty's right to have mercy upon those He sovereignly chose (Exodus 33:19) was not upon my first hearing a comforting declaration; there was, in fact, no guarantee that His mercy would triumph over His judgment. Real soul comfort only came when I saw the greatness of God's love for me, a sinful sinner, and how the lavishness of His love opened the way for me to become a son—a member of His very own family.

When H. G. Wells (*War of the Worlds*) was experiencing deep emotional distress his personal physician suggested that the cure might be found through the author's focusing his attention towards heaven and by seeking a relationship with the Almighty. Wells responded, 'I might just as well try shaking hands with the Milky Way.'

Yet, incredible though it may seem, I, like Abraham, can think of God as my Friend (James 2:23; John 16:27) and reach up to Him as my Father (Galatians 4:6). This intimacy, born solely of grace, teaches me that God's love for me rests entirely upon His accomplishments on my behalf: Christ's righteousness is truly mine simply through trusting in His self-sacrifice (2 Corinthians 5:21). My sonship stems from that relationship with Him (John 1:12), a relationship He has sovereignly initiated (John 17:6) and constantly maintains (John 10:28-29).

Embracing this truth, I need to dwell on it—as do we all—and draw refreshment from it every day. In this matter, what is true of me tends to be generally true of God's people: we are forever tending to lapse into some form of self-imposed legalism and forget that we cannot do anything to make God love us; and He will never love us any more than He does right now. After all, it was when we were enemies that He gave up His life for us (Romans 5:8-10).

Until we deepen in our awareness of the depths of His love for us, prayer will never become the vehicle for in-depth communion with our Father. Since our communication with God will inevitably be determined by our conception of Him, we must ask Him to rightly instruct our hearts and minds concerning His fathomless, unconditionally faithful love for us.

There are multitudes whose negative view of God—observe the misguided steward in Luke 19: 20-23—can only lead to woeful consequences. The chief demon in *The Screwtape Letters* tells his underling, 'It is funny how mortals always picture us as putting things into their minds: in reality our best work is done by keeping things out.'

We desperately need to be rooted and established in the knowledge of His love for us (Ephesians 3:17-19, cf. 1:17-19); it is so central to every aspect of our lives that we'll return to examine Paul's prayers for the Ephesians later on in this book.

THE PROBLEM OF FAITH

Virtually all prayer-related difficulties appear to have some link to faith; both the content and the extent of our prayers are wrapped up with our beliefs. If we don't understand the Bible's teaching on prayer (either through lack of effort or comprehension) the character of our faith will be greatly influenced by our emotions.

As a child I thought that if I stood on the top of my house I'd have better access to God since my elevated position set me so much closer to heaven. I actually tried praying from a neighbour's roof (mine was too perilous to ascend) and, with all the volume of which my small diaphragm was capable, launched a battery of words towards the billowy clouds above me. As I evaluate that event, Biblically, it seems fairly close to something that only the ancient adversaries of Israel would have thought reasonable (1 Kings 20:23,28).

FAITH IN GOD'S MESSAGE

Paul confirms the early believers in their relationship with Christ by insisting in the trustworthiness of that word of Christ which they had heard proclaimed (Romans 10:17). It was because they had believed what was told them that they had become God's children and received His Holy Spirit (Galatians 3:2,5). The very word which announced the great news of salvation by grace through faith also presented God's people with reliable teaching for their personal spiritual growth (2 Timothy 3:16).

Because all Scripture is God-breathed it is useful for teaching us about a variety of essential matters, including prayer. I suggest that our greatest prayer barrier is, ironically, something we have unwittingly erected; it is the unconscious result of our failure to study and embrace the Bible's revelation concerning prayer.

If there's one thing about which I'm certain it's this: Biblical reality must become my reality if my prayer life is to have the stature and dimensions intended by God. That reality declares that God loves me (John 16:27) —in spite of what I am, in spite of what I'm not. I must rest in that love, not in any imagined robustness of my prayers; mostly I am like the struggling father who cries out, 'I do believe; help me overcome my unbelief' (Mark 9:24)! He who had compassion on the son of an anxiety-ridden father still has pity on the weak, yet hopeful.

2
Learning To Listen

Early on in my Christian walk a spiritual friend told me, 'Prayer is asking and receiving.' While not untrue, the statement really had to do with only one aspect of prayer: the petitionary element. Surely the psalmist has much more than that in mind when he speaks of his thirst after God (63:1) and invites the people of Yahweh to 'taste' His unique goodness (34:8). We are often unwittingly like the youthful Samuel who is unaware of the richness of communion available to him until he cries out, 'Speak, Lord, for your servant is listening' (1 Samuel 3:10).

While a university student I often enjoyed hearing the Boston Symphony's musical director, Erich Leinsdorf, lead that superlative instrument in some of its richly diversified repertoire. During one particular concert the maestro turned unexpectantly to a shuffling, coughing audience and offered a mild rebuke: 'In today's presentation our contribution is the music; yours is silence—the blank tape upon which we will record our notes.'

I've found that I cannot do two things at the same time if one of them is listening. And, like so many others, I frequently find myself in a noisy environment—one over which I have no control. We are barraged with sounds—O, that dreadful

'Musak'— all the way from the elevator to the supermarket.

Strangely enough I often find myself more comfortable in that setting than in one characterized by the absence of sound. However, God says, 'Be still, and know that I am God' (Psalm 46:10); stillness is a prerequisite if we would deepen in our knowledge of Christ. Our stillness, itself, may serve as a vehicle for a deepening communion with God.

Although Israel's priest, Eli, critically misinterpreted Hannah's behaviour—he thought she was drunk—the dear woman was praying in her heart to the Lord (1 Samuel 1:13). Her unspoken prayer was heard. Perhaps her praying in silence better enabled her to discern God's presence as she 'poured her soul out to the Lord' (1 Samuel 1:15).

When evangelist George Whitefield observed God working powerfully through his preaching, he found himself so caught up with the wonder of God's marvellous work he recorded this appropriate response: 'After I came home I threw myself upon my bed and, in awful silence, admired the infinite freedom, sovereignty, and condescension of the love of God.'

Recently, on a clear summer's night I found myself gazing off into the star-clustered skies marvelling, too, at the splendour of the Almighty's work, an adumbration of His glory. Somehow I felt a strangely wonderful solidarity with Abraham who also must have viewed many of the same stars and saw them as a reminder of a majestic God's faithful promises (Genesis 15:5).

FILL IN THE BLANKS

Years ago a newspaper anecdote told of a woman of great culture who was entertaining guests at her formidable residence. The socialite was deploring the fact that, despite the fact that she had prayed religiously, she had never received an answer from the Almighty. How could one believe in Him? If He existed would she not have received some answer to the many requests she had addressed to Him over the past quarter century? 'Pardon, Madame,' responded one of her visitors, 'but did you ever leave Him time to get a word in?'

If we allow for the fact that prayer is like a two-way street, I need to follow Jesus' example of separating myself from noisy distractions and seek the Lord's Face (Luke 4:42; 6:12; cf. Psalm 27:8). I'm not suggesting, however, that we simply seek out a place of solitude, make our minds as blank as possible and wait for the Lord to reveal something to us. While God could do that if He so chose, He tells us that His wisdom is already crying out to us (Proverbs 8:1). His psalmist tells us to delight in letting the Scriptures fill our minds as we meditate upon God's word both day and night (Psalm 1:2).

According to a Gallup poll, two-thirds of those who called themselves evangelical (admittedly a term which needs to be qualified) said they didn't read the Bible regularly (although they recognized the desirability of doing so).

Paul tells the Corinthians that the true child of God actually has the mind of Christ (1 Corinthians 2:16). Whatever else this profound statement conveys, the apostle is saying that Christ, who had become Paul's wisdom (1 Corinthians 1:30), had given him His unerring and perfect word. It was through receiving that word that Paul had become wise in the things of God.

Remarkably, our having the mind of Christ rests on the identical foundation: letting His word richly dwell within us (Colossians 3:16). The results of making that word an integral part of your life affects not only your prayers but also your life as a whole. Spurgeon put it well, 'A Bible that's falling apart is usually owned by someone who isn't.'

'IT'S LONGER BUT IT'S SHORTER'

As a child I can recall my rabbi telling me a parable about a chap who desired to journey to a far country. A very wise man told him cryptically of two possible routes: one was shorter but longer; the other, longer but shorter. The lad chose the first of these only to realise that the road, while seemingly more direct, was virtually impassable due to the many obstacles along the way. Far easier to traverse was the lengthy road for it was well marked and most accommodating to travellers.

The rabbi was trying to motivate me to take the right road in life notwithstanding the time required for the journey. Nowhere is that principle more essential than in the matter of finding the route to a fulfilling prayer life. There's no short-cut to deep communion with God. E. M. Bounds said it well: 'God's acquaintance is not made hurriedly. He does not bestow His gifts on the casual or hasty comer and goer.'

If we want to grow in our knowledge of Him we'll have to spend time with the resource which uniquely presents His mind to ours. As a little boy learning to play the piano I often displeased my teacher because of my undisciplined, rather sporadic practising. In response to her spoken displeasure I remember my lame defence: 'I just don't have the time.' Her wise rejoinder has served to prod me for more than forty years: 'Stuart, you will always find time to do what's most important to you.'

We need to rethink our priorities. 'It is not' as Arthur Pink observed, 'because we are short of time, but because we lack a heart for the things of God.' What things are most worth pursuing? Although God offers us infinite joy we are, as C. S. Lewis observed, such 'half-hearted creatures', fooling around with meaningless things, 'like an ignorant child who wants to go on making mud pies in a slum because he cannot imagine what is meant by the offer of a holiday by the sea.'

I'm convinced that if we don't schedule time to pray it won't somehow just happen; what has been called the tyranny of the urgent will hold sway over us. Therefore, many of us need to ask God for a fresh resolve to establish time, as well as a place, to get alone with Him. Don't allow the press of the crowd or a frenetic lifestyle to keep you from life's most necessary pursuit (Psalm 105:4). You could start out simply by choosing a section of Scripture to read for guidance and asking the living, listening Source of it to help you grow in your understanding and personal application of it.

Ours is a Reader's Digest age; we like things condensed and easily assimilated. It seems we're always in a rush, finding little time for that unhurried devotion which characterized the psalmist's when he said, 'My eyes stay open through the watches of the night, that I may meditate on Your promises' (Psalm 119:148). I don't believe that the psalmist's experience was simply the result of his own determined efforts. Earlier he had asked Yahweh to turn him away from worthless things and towards God's word (119:36-37). The inspired author openly confessed his weariness as well as his need for strength and insight (vv. 28, 33-34). In his closing words God's servant acknowledges his lostness apart from the Lord's gracious intervention (v. 176).

Here is an Old Testament timeless glimpse of the work of the Holy Spirit, without whom none of us would either know or even faintly desire to seek the one true God. Dietrich Bonhoeffer's words are much to the point: 'I cannot pray alone, O God. In me there is darkness; but with Thee there is light.' The same Spirit who convicts us of our need is certainly prepared to meet that need within us.

DO TAKE IT PERSONALLY

We must not allow a veil of unreality to separate us from the personal message God has given us in His word. What Francis Schaeffer called 'true truth' is there to enable us to relate personally to God.

According to another Gallup poll, only 15% of the evangelical community read the Bible daily. Yet everything in the word is designed to spur us on to commune with our Lord. That's why Andrew Murray would regularly encourage Christians to read God's communication as in His very presence. 'Let it create around you and within you,' he would say, 'a holy atmosphere—a holy light—that you might be refreshed and strengthened.' When you read the word of God, do you take it personally or does it tend to be something more like an intellectual exercise?

Before the break-up of the Soviet Union I recall reading about an imprisoned Jewish activist who was forced to spend time in solitary confinement because he vehemently refused to relinquish his copy of the Psalms. Although we cannot know the motivation behind his stubbornness, one thing is certain: our personal recognition of the preciousness of God's word is essential if we want our relationship with Christ to truly flourish.

Meditating upon the Psalms helped me immeasurably when my life was falling apart. Sometimes in the disturbing silence late at night—when molehills more readily become mountains-I would read until my soul identified with the psalmist and received solace from that which God had given him to inscribe. That's surely not difficult to do; note how frequently some pressing trouble launches the psalmist to cry out!

While it's commendable to studiously take in sweeping portions of Scripture, I've found it enriching simply to focus on a verse or two for several days, asking the Holy Spirit to help me fully understand their content and deeply personalize them. Last week I focused on Matthew 6:27 where Jesus asks the question, 'Who of you by worrying can add a single hour to his life?' Considering Him whose days on earth were anything but bird-like or lily-like (verses 26, 28) helps me to accept the Master's teachings; His life makes credible His mandate to shun worrisome thoughts.

Concentrating on that text has caused me to thank God for His query which counters my tendency to indulge in anxious thoughts. In addition, that statement has compelled me to reflect on some of the many evidences of God's care for me and, as I do, cast my concerns upon the one truly faithful Rock of my life.

3
In The Dark

'Christian faith,' according to C. S. Lewis, 'does not start with joy, but rather with despair; and you cannot bypass the despair in an attempt to reach the joy.' Although animals do not experience despair, neither can they know hope. Hope comes to him who has worked through his despair in the light of the gospel; only then may he receive a hope which does not disappoint and find encouragement (Romans 5:5; Hebrews 6:18).

Peter tells the church to cast all anxiety upon Christ because of His watchful care (1 Peter 5:7). Easier said than done. Sometimes anxiety hangs over you like a shroud. When, after fourteen years of ministry, my church elders asked me to find employment elsewhere I was crushed. When my unmarried daughter conceived a child I was deeply distraught. Peanut's Charlie Brown was wrong when he said there was no problem so deep or severe that it could not be run away from.

Moses tells us that prior to God's revealing His covenantal provisions to Abram, 'a thick and dreadful darkness came over him' (Genesis 15:12). How strange that the prelude to wonderful words of promise should be so fearfully unpleasant.

We have all known the stressful perplexity of Dante's cry, 'I woke up in the middle of the woods and it was dark and there was no clear way before me.' It is in such distressful times that we'd welcome 'a deep sleep' (Genesis 15:12). When David found himself maligned and mistreated - by someone he thought was his friend - he uttered a phrase which the Spirit may very well have used to influence Peter's statement:

Cast your cares on the Lord
and He will sustain you ... (Psalm 55:22)

The King James Version reads 'burden' for the New International's Version 'cares' which comes from a Hebrew root meaning 'that which is given'. The burden you now bear - whatever it is - comes to you as a gift from a sovereign God. He who gives it to you invites you to offer it up to Him, if you will, as an offering - a sacrifice.

WHO'S PRAYING NOW?

David Jacobsen, an American held hostage in Beirut for a year and a half, was chained, ill-fed, and cruelly abused. He and his fellow inmates, who founded what they ruefully called 'the Church of the Locked Door', would clasp hands and cry out to God for help. Jacobsen said that it was in that dismal cell that the Holy Spirit showed him that 'when the Holy Comforter is called, He answers'.

Yet dreadful darkness comes in many forms and may debilitate even the strongest Christian. There come times which are so unsettling or disorienting that we simply find ourselves unable to pray.

David Brainerd, one of the brightest missionary lights in the colonies at the time of the Great Awakening, recorded these candid reflections in his diary: 'Was scarce able to walk about, and was obliged to betake myself to bed ... and passed away the time ... being neither able to read, meditate, nor pray ... O how heavily does time pass away, when I can do nothing to any good purpose; but seem obliged to trifle away precious time.' This is the same spiritual giant who regularly spoke of his passionate devotion for Christ and of his dedicated prayer life.

Forgive me if this seems to border on heresy but it would not surprise me at all, had the apostle Paul kept a diary, to read that even this most extraordinary saint experienced 'off' times not unlike those of Brainerd's. It's hard to imagine that Paul's beatings, shipwrecks, sleepless nights, contentious brethren and severe deprivations never exerted a negative effect on his prayerfulness. Of course this is conjectural.

But what is not uncertain is the immediate value that Paul ascribes to his suffering. 'Who is weak, and I do not feel weak?' (2 Corinthians 11:29). Through his crises Paul's empathy was enlarged, thereby widening the sphere of his ministry's influence. And he takes it a step further, realising that his weakness drives him to trust in God 'that Christ's power may rest on me' (2 Corinthians 12:9). Indeed, the sufferings appeared to serve as the vehicle delivering an unearthly empowerment to minister God's comfort to others in trouble (2 Corinthians 1:3-5).

In Thornton Wilder's play, *The Angel That Troubled the Pool*, someone is about to enter into the waters of a pool as they begin to stir; yet an angel stops him, saying, 'Without your wound, where would your power be?' Another who has just been healed approaches the one whose healing has been denied and implores him to minister to his disturbed son, 'Come with me to my home; my son is lost in dark thoughts and I do not understand him ...'. It was because of the unrelieved pain and suffering of the one refused healing that he could effectively reach out to another in need, as the angel pointedly declares, 'In love's service only the wounded soldiers can serve.'

In rabbinical debate, a popular ancient method, called *pilpul*, is still employed by scholars today as a teaching device. Unlike the Socratic method where a teacher asks a student a question, one teacher will state a proposition and another will show why it is incorrect. The first speaker will then respond to the second's criticism and so it goes, back and forth, until, in this rather gracious form of polemic, either the rabbis or their listeners are exhausted.

There's a good deal of hair-splitting in these sessions, many of which are recorded in the Talmud. Sometimes the subjects of these debates are of little importance; at other times, however, we may overhear, as it were, soul-searching dialogue. Consider one of these debated questions: 'Does God love more the person who has sinned and repented or the person who has never sinned?' The debate concludes with the weight of the argument favouring the one who has never sinned, in contrast to Jesus' teaching that there is no rejoicing over these (Luke 15:7).

Another meaty question had to do with the sufferer: 'Why did God permit the Godly to experience such great sorrows?' The resolution to that discussion had little in common with Aristotelian logic, for in rabbinic debate two seemingly contradictory statements could stand side by side. So it was, with special reference to Job, that this conclusion was reached: 'The one whom God loves much receives riches but the one whom God loves most is allowed to suffer.' Isaiah tells us that God the Father put His Son to grief (Isaiah 53:10); it was through the Messiah's sufferings that He became the perfect Saviour for us (Hebrews 5:8-9).

It is through our sorrows that God may reveal His love to us—and through us to others—in a manner otherwise unknowable. God gives you what orthodox Jews call *tzuris* (trouble) in order to use you for the good of others. Elisabeth Elliot remembers a college speaker expressing it this way: 'If my life is broken when given to Jesus it may be because pieces will feed a multitude when a loaf would satisfy only a little boy.'

There is no time that trust in Christ's benevolent power is more important than when, like Brainerd, you are unable to pray, when it is as if your tongue sticks to the roof of your mouth (Psalm 22:15). Because God has given you His Holy Spirit, who by His own initiative has become an integral part of your life, there is within you a recurring, if not always unwavering, conviction that your heavenly Father loves you (John 16:27); that love has made provision for what the Spanish mystic, John of the Cross, called 'the dark night of the soul'. Though you may be imprisoned and bound by silence, the Holy Spirit is never inarticulate; He is committed to help you in your weakness and intercedes for you, praying perfectly on your behalf in accordance with God's will (Romans 8:26-27). In these marvellous verses Paul is telling the church that, in order to keep them in vital communication with their God, the Holy Spirit acts quite independently of their efforts and does so flawlessly.

When John Newton, author of the hymn *Amazing Grace*, saw his cancer-ridden wife dying a slow and painful death, he found himself pacing about, offering disjointed prayers from a grief-torn heart. Then somewhere deep in his soul he felt the stirrings of the Spirit who helped him recall the reliable promises of God. Newton cried out, 'Lord, I am helpless indeed, in myself, but hope I am willing, without reserve, that Thou shouldest help me.'

Our cries for help as well as all uplifting remembrances must be identified as the work of the Holy Spirit who is intent upon kindling within us all things necessary to our peace (John 14:26-27). He comes to us to prevent us from being swallowed up by the fear of being abandoned (2 Corinthians 4:9); oh, for the grace to respond fully to His loving overtures that our deepest thirsts may be assuaged.

One of Soren Kierkegaard's prayers is a poignantly beautiful reminder of the fact that His restorative initiative is designed to induce a longing in our souls for His fellowship —a yearning that He will surely satisfy (see, especially, Psalm 63):

> Father in heaven, well we know that it is Thou that giveth both to will and to do; that also longing, when it leads us to renew the fellowship with our Saviour and Redeemer, is from Thee. Father in heaven, longing is Thy gift. But when longing lays hold of us, oh that we might lay hold of the longing! When it would carry us away, that we also might give ourselves up! When Thou art near to summon us, that we also in prayer might stay near Thee! When Thou in the longing dost offer us the highest good, oh, that we might hold it fast!

Of course, when you are raw and hurt and bleeding, you may not find the support you desire to be immediately at hand. No one knew that better than C. S. Lewis who had to come to grips with what appeared to be heaven's indifference to the bone cancer that would excruciatingly claim his wife's life. It was as if a door had been slammed in his face, bolted, and double-bolted on the inside. In those desperate times Lewis knew 'that even the fingernails of hands folded in prayer could be bitten to the quick.'

Yet ultimately we are, by God's sovereign grace, drawn back to those invaluable truths which are designed to undergird us: chiefly, that we are loved not because of who we are, but because of who God is. Author Victor Hugo found that life's greatest happiness comes to us through the conviction that we are really loved — 'loved, as it were, in spite of ourselves'.

Covenant love is like that; its commitment does not rest on the faithfulness of the one loved; it 'does not alter when it alteration finds'. We are so used to dealing with one another on a contractual basis — 'I do this for you if you do that for me' — that it's unnatural for us to think of a loving commitment which holds deep and steady in the face of our inconstancy. What splendid evidence we have of God's unwavering commitment: Jesus Christ has joined us in our sorrows; He was profoundly hurt and bled and wept; a Man of sorrows who knows all there is to know about grief in its multiple forms; He has promised never to leave us (even when our senses bombard us with thoughts to the contrary). This Lord, has come, as George MacDonald says, 'to wipe away our tears. He is doing it; He will have it done as soon as He can; and until He can, He would have them flow without bitterness ...'.

There have been times when intense sorrow has left me feeling dejected — without a prayer. Although none of us is exempt from the effect of emotional havoc on his spiritual zeal, we have a Saviour who empathizes with us in our weakness and who lives forever to make intercession for us (Hebrews 4:15; 7:25). His attitude doesn't change towards us when we fail to pray, or pray sporadically, or pray ill-advisedly. This is an effective antidote to poisonous despair; it's the best way to emerge from that darkness which may threaten to engulf us. *His* faithfulness will ultimately win the day.

Corrie ten Boom believed it even in the benighted death camp of Ravensbruk; ' However deep the pit,' she said, 'God's love is deeper still.'

In His extremity, He who suffered in our place soon found

His hope renewed (Psalm 22:1, compare with verse 24); and because of His victory we, too, may have confidence and come boldly into the welcoming presence of Him who said, 'Whoever comes to me I will never drive away' (John 6:37).

O Thou, the contrite sinner's Friend,
Who, loving, lovest to the end,
On this alone my hopes depend,
That Thou wilt plead for me.

When, weary in the Christian race,
Far off appears my resting-place,
And, fainting, I mistrust Thy grace,
Then, Saviour, plead for me.

When I have erred and gone astray,
Afar from Thine and wisdom's way,
And see no glimmering, guiding ray,
Still, Saviour, plead for me.

When Satan, by my sins made bold,
Strives from Thy cross to loose my hold,
Then with Thy pitying arms enfold,
And plead, oh, plead, for me.

When the full light of heavenly day
Reveals my sins in dread array,
Say, Thou hast washed them all away;
Dear Saviour, plead for me.

(Charlotte Elliott, 1789-1871)

4
Who's Listening Now?

For the German philosopher, Immanuel Kant, prayer was little more than a superstitious illusion. For the rebellious king Ahaz, God's offer to hear his prayer revealed both the monarch's hypocrisy and God's disdain for his feigned spirituality (Isaiah 6:10-13).

As a teenager I found myself in trouble with the law and had to stand before a judge who was trying to determine an appropriate sentence for me. Before announcing his judgment he asked me, 'How may I know that you will never again have to stand before me?' From the look on his face my answer must have surprised him. 'Your honour,' I said nervously, 'I've prayed with my rabbi concerning this problem and have promised God never to offend Him in this way again.' Somehow that was acceptable to the magistrate who discerned that, for me, prayer was neither an illusion nor a vehicle for hypocrisy.

Yet as I try to remember my experience with my rabbi, I don't recall having asked God for the grace necessary to keep that vow. My attitude may have been as presumptuous as that implicit in my forbears' bold promise when Moses confronted them with God's law —'We will do everything the Lord has said' (Exodus 19:7-8). Notwithstanding, His grace did keep me out of further trouble, at least with the local courts.

Many years would pass before I began to comprehend His genuine concern for me as my heavenly Father. It is something about which I still have much to learn. More and more I have become conscious of the unseen Hand of divine providence. God is unceasingly working in all things for His own glory and the well-being of His people; and it's a first principle that He's always doing something concerning your life long before you have any knowledge of it.

The Puritan, John Flavel, took special delight in that truth, desiring to persuade Christians of its wonderful relevance, noting, 'With what profound wisdom, infinite tenderness and incessant vigilance [Providence] has managed all that concerns us from first to last.'

The God of providence is the God who provides. He was called *Yahweh Yireh* by Abraham on the occasion of his sacrificial provision for Isaac on Mount Moriah (Genesis 22:14). The great comfort bound up with that expression is simply this: 'Seeing [our needs], God provides.' What happened on Moriah bore witness to God's perfect provision in the death of His Son on Mount Calvary, the latter event testifying also to His exhaustive care for us (Romans 8:32, Philippians 4:19).

So our prayers must never be thought of as an effort to wrest our needs from One who is in any way indifferent or capricious; neither is he, as John Calvin put it, 'winking or sleeping until aroused by the sound of our voice.'

We need to realize, however, that Providence also is in charge of life's painful experiences. The prophets repeatedly acknowledge God as the author of the hard times as well as the pleasant ones (Isaiah 45:7; Lamentations 3:32). These distressing events are also exercised in love; His invincible power causes even the most bitter experience to yield good for us (Genesis 50:20; Romans 8:28)–to ultimately, as Professor Berkouwer said, 'turn it to our profit.'

DAVIDIC TUTORIAL

When David penned Psalm 139 he was tremendously moved by a divinely-given awareness of the majesty of his omniscient God. Nothing could hide the psalmist from the all-seeing eye of God; the minutest of David's actions were all known to the Lord.

Much more than that, however, David was conscious of the fact that God perceived all of his thoughts (v.2) and knew what he was going to say even before the words were uttered (v.4). God's comprehensive knowledge of David transcended time and space (v.15-16); it was mind-boggling for David — 'too wonderful' ... 'too lofty' (v.6).

But if God knows every word we're going to say before we speak, why bother to articulate thoughts the Almighty already discerns? Perhaps the oral expression is basically for our benefit, that we may be fully conscious of the things we are entrusting to His care—the matters which we know we cannot face without divine aid. Our petitions pay Him the honour due Him by acknowledging the fact that all we receive comes from above (James 1:17). The words which we utter serve to unveil the thoughts of our hearts; as concerning God they make patently clear both the character of our worship and the degree of our dependency.

While some aspects of prayer are shrouded in mystery God has undeniably purposed to use our prayers as the means whereby He accomplishes His will; He is committed to perform His gracious will through our petitions, requests which the Holy

Spirit, Himself, motivates us to make. This holds true whether we are praying on a wide or a small scale, whether we utter a plea for societal justice or for personal development (Psalm 139:19,23).

Do you think of yourself as a child who is always under the watchful care of the Almighty God? If so, doesn't it stand to reason that your prayer life should be influenced by that persuasion? It is fitting for us to echo David's glad thoughts in a spirit of praise: 'You discern my going out and my lying down; You are familiar with all my ways... You hem me in—behind and before; You have laid Your hand upon me' (Psalm 139:3,5).

LESS SELF-ABSORPTION

On the occasion of my baptism thirty years ago the pastor gave me a copy of John Baillie's *Diary of Private Prayer*. Once chaplain to the Queen of Scotland, his prayers, designed to stimulate the devotions of others, have a special selfless quality—they don't get bogged down extensively in self-absorbed petitions; instead, they focus on the One who always fulfils His purposes for His child (Psalm 57:2). Consider the tone and content of one typical prayer:

'Here am I, O God, of little power and of mean estate, yet lifting up heart and voice to Thee before whom all created things are as dust and a vapour. Thou art hidden behind the curtain of sense, incomprehensible in Thy greatness, mysterious in Thine almighty power; yet here I speak with Thee familiarly as child to parent, as friend to friend. If I could not thus speak to Thee, then were I indeed without hope in the world. For it is little that I have power to do or to ordain. Not of my own will am I here, not of my own will shall I soon pass hence. Of all that shall come to me this day, very little will be such as I have chosen for myself. It is Thou, O hidden One, who dost appoint my lot and determine the bounds of my habitation. It is Thou who hast put power in my hand to do one work and hast withheld the skill to do another. It is Thou who dost keep in Thy grasp the threads of this day's life and alone knowest what lies before me to do or to suffer. But because Thou art my Father, I am not afraid. Because it is Thine own Spirit that stirs within my spirit's inmost room, I know that all is well. What I desire for myself I cannot attain, but what Thou desirest in me Thou canst attain for me. The good that I would do I do not, but the good that Thou willest in me, that Thou canst give me power to do.'

I've delighted in the worshipper's recognition of his weakness in stark contrast to the sovereign rule of his almighty Lord, a sensitivity leading to the many soul-edifying affirmations of his prayer. There follows immediately a joyful submissiveness to his Father's will:

'Dear Father, take this day's life into Thine own keeping. Control all my thoughts and feelings. Direct all my energies. Instruct my mind. Sustain my will. Take my hands and make them skilful to serve Thee. Take my feet and make them swift to do Thy bidding. Take my eyes and keep them fixed upon Thine everlasting beauty. Take my mouth and make it eloquent in testimony to Thy love. Make this day a day of obedience, a day of spiritual joy and peace. Make this day's work a little part of the work of the Kingdom of my Lord Christ, in whose name these my prayers are said. Amen.'

I have regularly had the opportunity to bring the gospel to groups of Muslims who, in characteristic Islamic fashion, would periodically break off from their conversation to submissively prostrate themselves before Allah in prayer (by definition, a Muslim is one who submits). Yet I've never discerned any joy in those acts of submission, perhaps because they do not see God as their heavenly Father whose will is designed to bring joy to the hearts of His people. It is one thing to submit to a king because of His absolute might; it is quite another thing to yield to His will because you know it encompasses your needs and is paternally benevolent.

Baillie's prayer recognizes the distinct privilege which is ours: to actually bring glory to God by serving Him in the unique situation which He has tailor-made for each of His children. He opens the door to unparalleled joy to all who desire His will and follow His way. We have been deluded by our emotions—run rough-shod over by the world—to believe that real contentment can only be achieved through material means.

Before billionaire H. Ross Perot entered the 1993 presidential race, *Fortune* magazine quoted him as saying: 'Guys, just remember, if you get real lucky, if you make a lot of money, if you go out and buy a lot of stuff—it's gonna break. You got your biggest, fanciest mansion in the world. It has air conditioning. It's got a pool. Just think of all the pumps that are going to go out. Or go to a yacht basin any place in the world. Nobody is smiling, and I'll tell you why. Something broke that morning. The generator's out; the microwave doesn't work ... *Things* just don't mean happiness.'

Far too many Christians have been duped into believing a lie; like the ancients they are 'intent on pursuing worthless things' (Hosea 5:11). Consequently the real value of their lives is obscured and their prayers misshapen by a worldly perspective.

LET'S BE REAL!

Genuine worship does not consist in offering up elaborate prayers or reciting impressive liturgies; real worship is nothing less than the offering of ourselves up to God. It is not only our reasonable, spiritual worship (Romans 12:1); it is the only true foundation for our personal joy and fulfilment.

When it seems that I haven't got a prayer I need to look to God for that true spirit of worship spoken of so insightfully by Archbishop William Temple:

> Worship is the submission of all our nature to God: it is the quickening of conscience by His holiness; the nourishment of mind with His truth; the purifying of imagination by His beauty; the opening of the heart to His love; the surrender of will to His purpose—and all this gathered up in adoration, the most selfless emotion of which our nature is capable and therefore the chief remedy for that self-centredness which is our original sin and the source of all actual sin.

According to Jeremiah 31:32, the history of Israel was lived out under a broken covenant: 'They broke My covenant and I had to lord it over them'—I had to treat them as if I was a slave owner. Only the grace of God's New Covenant can transform service into an occasion for joy and thankful praise. Unless we sense the greatness of His undeserved favour we shall forever be like the pathetic elder son who told his father, 'All these years I've been slaving for you' (Luke 15:29).

If we cannot find words of thanks for our God we simply haven't understood the incomparable work of Christ on our behalf. In a letter to his son, Puritan Thomas Goodwin revealed how reflecting upon what Christ had accomplished served to revive his flagging zeal:

When I was threatening to become cold in my ministry and when I felt Sabbath morning coming and my heart not filled with amazement at the grace of God, or when I was making ready to dispense the Lord's Supper, do you know what I used to do? I used to take a turn up and down among the sins of my past life and I always came down again with a broken and contrite heart... And many a Sabbath morning, when my soul had been cold and dry for the lack of prayer during the week, a turn up and down in my past life before I went into the pulpit always broke my hard heart and made me close with the gospel for my own soul...

Those who speak of His grace or offer words of loving devotion to God must do so in response to His initiative; they know they have been made the objects of His lavish love, a love that compels them to somehow reciprocate (1 John 3:1; 4:19).

MY LIFE, A PRAYER
There is a sense in which the offering of our lives up to God is a non-verbal prayer, an expression of worship well-pleasing to God (Romans 12:1). It is never more precious than when it is offered up in times of trouble—in times when we are perplexed but will not allow despair to tyrannize us (2 Corinthians 4:8).

Somewhere in *Screwtape's Letters* the elder tempter observes how his cause to defeat a Christian is never in greater jeopardy than when such a person looks about him, sees nothing to convince him of God's present care yet, notwithstanding, seeks to obey his Lord. In her penetrating video series, *Suffering is Not for Nothing*, Elisabeth Elliot observes that there is no consolation to compare with obedience. She points to Ezekiel who did just as he was commanded to do, even though death suddenly claimed 'the delight of his eyes' --his wife (Ezekiel 24:15-18).

The noblest form of worship is obedience (I Samuel 15:22). When we do what we believe is pleasing to God (in spite of the most formidable obstacles), there comes a peace which passes understanding. And when we seek to do His will, however difficult that may be, we may be able to say with the patriarch Joseph, 'God has caused me to be fruitful in the land of my affliction' (Genesis 41:52). Eventually every child of God will affirm the underlying truth which Isaac Watt's much beloved hymn expressed so well: 'Love so amazing, so divine, demands my soul, my life, my all.'

When Elisabeth Elliot was a young girl she copied in the back of her Bible a prayer of visiting missionary Betty Scott Stam who, along with her husband, would one day be executed in China because of their witness for Christ. Her written prayer serves as a powerful testimony to a mature woman of God:

Lord, I give up all my own plans and purposes, all my own desires and hopes, and accept Thy will for my life. I give myself, my life, my all, utterly to Thee to be Thine forever. Fill me and seal me with Thy Holy Spirit, use me as Thou wilt, send me where Thou wilt, work out Thy whole will in my life at any cost, now and forever.

5
Breaking Faith

Few of us could deny what Richard Newton called 'an unaccountable backwardness to prayer'. This is revealed not only in our prayerlessness but also in our hypocrisy. There are innumerable folk who truly pray what's on their mind but they're self-deceived. 'I thank you that I'm not like other men,' the religious leader prayed (Luke 18:11). His darkened heart spoke what he believed but what he said was a lie.

For years I prayed with at least a subconscious notion that my sins were mere peccadilloes. Certainly, I thought, I was no worse than my fellow synagogue worshipper—better than some. The true state of what one expositor called my 'Babylonian' heart was unknown to me. It was grace that made me aware of the truth about myself and prompted me to cry out to the One who alone could save me from that devastating eternity to which my sin justly consigned me. 'It is a good day,' a Puritan prayed, 'when Thou givest me a glimpse of myself.'

There are times, however, when I find it difficult to speak the truth to my God. My glimpse of self is something I choose to squelch because I sense it would be entirely unacceptable to Him. I want to present myself as I ought to be, not as I am. So I wear the hypocrite's mask and speak words untrue to what I'm thinking and feeling.

Maimonides, a 12th century Jewish scholar, taught that our love of God will be proportionate to our knowledge of Him. Shortly after coming to trust in my Messiah, Jesus, I was invited to speak at a synagogue in my home town. It was a wintry New England Sabbath day when I shared with the people of Temple Israel the reasons I had come to faith in 'Yeshuah'. Chief among the blessings, I pointed out, was the fulfilment of Yahweh's covenantal promise to Jeremiah, 'They will all know Me, from the least of them to the greatest' (Jeremiah 31:34).

In nearly three hours of debate this was the only point in time when the chief spiritual representative for the congregation expressed his sympathetic appreciation of my presentation. He acknowledged that the goal of true religion was to know God—to know Him intimately, as Jeremiah prophesied. Jeremiah's foretaste of that intimacy was characterized by the openness—the frankness—of his words to God (cf. Jeremiah 20:7).

Yet my knowledge of Him has not been characterized by an uninterrupted, intimate fellowship. Recurring frustrations and disappointments, not to mention personal sin, have all taken their toll on that 'mystic sweet communion' about which so many of us have had occasion to sing. Furthermore, I must confess to having a regrettably limited understanding of His extremely patient love towards me. As a result I've often found it difficult to speak my heart's true sentiments before Him; I've not trusted God enough to be honest with Him.

SPEAKING THE TRUTH IN ANGUISH

Maggie Ross tells us about a survivor of the Holocaust named Emma who daily stood outside a Manhattan church screaming insults at Jesus. Finally the pastor came to her and said, 'Why don't you go inside and tell Him?' She slipped into the sanctuary. After an hour the minister, a bit fearful for her well-being, peeked in on Emma only to find her lying prostrate before the cross. He reached down and touched her shoulder. She looked up and, with tearful eyes, said in a hushed voice, 'After all, he was a Jew, too.' Somehow Emma may have begun to penetrate the mystery of His ways.

Is it ever acceptable for Christians to express their anger before their heavenly Father? Joni Eareckson Tada, having been paralysed from a diving accident, was seething with anger and chose to launch her venomous barbs at anyone near her since God seemed to be inaccessible. Would she have deeply offended the Lord by expressing her bitter spirit before Him?

Before judging such behaviour 'unspiritual', it would be worthwhile to hear Job's lament: 'Is my complaint directed to man? Why should I not be impatient' (Job 21:4)? 'Even today my complaint is bitter; His hand is heavy in spite of my groaning' (Job 23:2). The patriarch could not suppress his groanings, even recognizing their rebelliousness (reading 'rebellious' for the NIV's 'bitter'). What is astounding about Job is that he considers the possibility that God takes pleasure in oppressing him (10:3) and even asks God to leave him alone (7:19). The fact that the Holy Spirit has preserved Job's anguished candour in Scripture should encourage us to say what's really on our mind; God is obviously big enough to handle it.

How does He whom Job calls *Shaddai* (Almighty) respond to His child? Perhaps unexpectantly we hear Him tell Job's miserable comforters, 'You have not spoken of Me what is right, as My servant Job has' (42:7). Although God is not vindicating every word spoken by Job, He is nonetheless witnessing to the integrity of His servant. Job will have nothing to do with facades.

Since God knows His child's thoughts there's no point in trying to hide or disguise them, even when they're far from what we believe we ought to express. I'd like to be able to go about saying 'Hallelujah' all the time but God knows my heart would be out of tune with my voice. Let's be honest: no one can always have devout feelings; and our feelings are not God's primary concerns. We are always on far more solid ground when we focus on His love for us rather than ours for Him.

If God is as loving as He is almighty (and Scripture affirms that to be so) we wonder why He allows so many distressing events to unsettle our lives. Sometimes they come with such intensity that we find ourselves either unable to pray or mouthing insincere platitudes which are as detached from us as a five-year-old's singing 'Years I spent in vanity and pride...'. Elisabeth Elliot is right when she says that 'Faith's most severe tests come not when we see nothing, but when we see a stunning array of evidence that seems to prove our faith vain.'

LET IT SUFFICE THEE

Moses' life's objective was bound up with Canaan; a third of his life was spent in pursuit of that promised land. But an earlier, hot-tempered act would disallow his crossing the Jordan. What must have been especially upsetting to Moses was the fact that he had pleaded with Him whom he had known as a friend to allow his passage into the land (Deuteronomy 3:23-25). His prayer was a logical culmination to his forty years' quest, offered hopefully, humbly, sincerely. The KJV has God responding with the words, 'Let it suffice thee.' Having spent one-third of his life in pursuit of Palestine, the words must have been hard to hear. Perhaps you, too, find God's seemingly brusque response somewhat troubling.

THE DIVINE DENOUEMENT

Many years prior to this event Moses had made another request of God: 'Teach me your ways so I may know you' (Exodus 33:13). Moses was to find that some prayers are answered in unimaginable ways. Getting to know God better meant that Moses had to live under the same law as his people, a law that would not leave the guilty unpunished (Exodus 34:7). There was an unavoidable consequence stemming from Moses' ill-tempered behaviour when he unwittingly diminished the Israelites' perception of Yahweh's glory (Numbers 20:10).

On the positive side, however, God had something better in store for Moses. Rather than leading a stubborn people into a land soon to be polluted by their sin, Moses was to have his deepest desires met: to behold God in His splendour and enjoy Him, incorruptible, forever.

The Scriptures convince me that God has a hidden agenda for each of us; He has purposed to do and permit many things which we will perceive to be anything but pleasant. Although we applaud the subtleties of a Faulkner or a Proust, we strangely assume that God must be direct and obvious as He works in our lives. While His actions may be inscrutable, His stated goal for us is clear: to make us like His Son and bring us to glory (Hebrews 2:10).

In studying the life of our Lord it becomes evident that His obedience was not enhanced by the many miracles He performed but, rather, by the things He suffered (Hebrews 5:8). Should not all of God's chosen instruments expect to find a parallel between their lives and His? (Acts 9:15-16). The way He answers our prayers must ultimately relate to His unalterable intention to make us like Christ and enable us to enjoy Him forever.

I had only been a Christian for a few months when I received word from a former music teacher that his wife was dying from cancer. In a dream I sensed that God was motivating me to travel to his distant residence and pray for Dorine's healing. When I arrived Ed greeted me warmly and hopefully; I had shared with him my burden for his wife. As I saw her emaciated form in the bed where she had helplessly lain, my spirits sank low. She was so far gone; how could I pray in faith, believing? Yet I did what I came to do: gently touching her delicate arm I asked for her healing.

Months later, at a time of intense and upsetting opposition from members of my family, I sadly opened a letter from my friend, Ed, whose situation I had all but forgotten due to my domestic difficulties. I shall never forget what God did that day. At just the right time I received word of His miracle in the life of Dorine, whose return to health had baffled her doctors.

The unexpected news gave me new hope and a fresh resolve to follow my Messiah; it also taught me that God is not limited by my less-than-vibrant faith or my ability to figure out how He could meet a vexing need. I must guard against adopting the mindset of the officer who responded doubtingly to Elisha's promise of abundance, 'Look, even if the Lord should open the floodgates of the heavens, could this happen' (2 Kings 7:2)?

Decades have passed since the day of that act of God and, although I've prayed many times for the sick, nothing like that event has taken place again. In his *Knowing God*, J. I. Packer points out that, with very young Christians, the start of their spiritual lives is often marked by extraordinary answers to prayer; 'thus God encourages and establishes them' in Christ.

But as they mature He builds their character by exercising them in a tougher school, exposing them to tests and pressures unknown to them in the earliest days of their new life. All of God's children may expect this type of treatment for God declares it to be normative (Acts 14:22; Hebrews 12:5). In the face of life's perceived tragedies we can trust Him that, no matter what happens to us, His unerring plan for each of us is good, for He is good. And, as the immensely tested patriarch, Job, decisively proved, God is in the business of blessing His children. Even in the bleakest of situations nothing can affect His stated purpose to bless, not curse (Jeremiah 29:11-13); 'We have this hope as an anchor for the soul, firm and secure ...' (Hebrews 6:19).

A PRAYER OF ONE PERPLEXED

My Lord God, I have no idea where I am going. I do not see the road ahead of me. I cannot know for certain where it will end. Nor do I really know myself, and the fact that I think that I am following Your will does not mean that I am actually doing so. But I believe that the desire to please You does in fact please You. And I hope I have that desire in all that I am doing. I hope that I will never do anything apart from that desire. And I believe that if I do this You will be pleased with me though I may know nothing about it. Therefore will I trust You always; though I may seem to be lost and in the shadow of death, I will not fear, for You are ever with me, and You will never leave me to face my perils alone.

Anonymous

6
The Uphill Struggle

Rachmiel, a Jewish colleague who survived a Nazi concentration camp, loved to share his favourite Bible verse, one that had been his focal point during the Holocaust: '...weeping may remain for a night, but rejoicing comes in the morning' (Psalm 30:5). He used to love to read his copy of the ancient Hebrew Scriptures (without the vowel pointings) and say them aloud in order to gain their full impact. More important, He persisted to pray in the light of God's Word in spite of unrelenting problems and seemingly insurmountable odds; and the things God taught him in the darkness, as Fenelon said, he would 'forever retain'.

Jesus taught his disciples to pray and never give up (Luke 18:1). Yet prayer is, in the words of E. M. Bounds, 'taxing, spiritual work'. By virtue of its demanding nature, we tend to avoid an in-depth commitment to the work of prayer. We become discouraged so easily. Perhaps it's because we live in a time when people want quick answers—instant gratification—and are particularly adverse to waiting patiently for anything. We're in such a hurry that we even tend to morally congratulate ourselves when we let another motorist enter the stream of traffic in front of us. But if our lassitude and impatience discourage praying we must acknowledge that a more basic obstacle is sin itself.

A Puritan's reflections speak well for me: 'O God, Thou injured, neglected, provoked benefactor, when I think upon Thy greatness and Thy goodness I am ashamed at my insensibility; I blush to lift up my face, for I have foolishly erred.' Mark Twain was right when he said, 'Man is the only animal that blushes --- or needs to!'

Yet here I'm not thinking so much of our 'generic' sin which gives rise to a spiritual weariness and restlessness; I'm referring to those oft-repeated specific thoughts and acts which tend to make us want to hide from God. Although we give lip service to the fact that repentant confession restores the sweetness of our fellowship with God (1 John 1:9), in practice we are often so disgusted with ourselves we sulk and find it hard to believe that nothing 'will be able to separate us from the love of God that is in Christ Jesus our Lord' (Romans 8:39). As a result we allow our own misguided conscience to occlude our prayers; we let our emotions, rather than the Scriptures, control our actions.

DEALING WITH TREACHEROUS THOUGHTS

Shakespeare wrote, 'our doubts are traitors'; yet each of us has owned thoughts belying his confession of faith. Isaiah was sensitive to his people's discouragement. They were of an opinion that God's disciplinary acts were devoid of loving concern. To be sure, many needed to turn to God and, with deep contrition, turn from ways which were offensive to Him. Until they did, it was as if God did not hear their cries (Isaiah 59:1-2).

But among those upon whom God had placed His gracious hand, many were saying, 'My way is hidden from the Lord; my cause is disregarded by my God' (Isaiah 40:27). They had lost touch with reality. It was not God's intention to abandon the work of His hands; neither was He detached from their personal problems. So His prophet reminds the people that they should continue to hope in the Lord who will renew their strength (v.31). 'He who believes will not panic' (Isaiah 28:16b, author's translation).

Isaiah knew how God's wonderful provision from the altar had provided an atonement which allowed him, a defiled sinner, to enter into the presence of God (6:5-7). That experience should be normative for each of us in the sense that Jesus' priceless work on the cross—the anticipation of the Old Testament's atoning sacrifices—has ushered us into the presence of God Himself, who will never cast us away (John 6:37; Ephesians 1:3).

From that vantage point our trials tend to assume a less formidable posture. Once again we are challenged to accept the teaching of Scripture over the murmurings of our battered emotions. The necessity is to embrace these convictions deeply within our hearts. If you have come to a place in your life where, like Israel, you feel God has left you high and dry, let the clear teaching of the Word take precedence over your doubts; ask God for the grace to believe what is written.

Luther criticized Erasmus telling him that his thoughts of God were 'too human'. That's exactly our problem as well. For example, we are often reluctant to take small matters to Him, thinking of God as some very busy, overworked executive who couldn't possibly have the time or inclination to deal with our everyday problems. But He never grows weary and delights in responding to the appeals of the weak (Isaiah 40: 28-29). We make our evaluations on naive impulses rather than on the truthfulness of God's sure revelation.

In the Talmud the rabbis say that in heaven God will ask His people if they had a set time for study; therefore the venerable rabbi Simeon taught his disciples, 'Let your studies be fixed.' Without a fixed time for studying the Bible each of us is quite vulnerable to a pessimistic view of God, His care for us, and His provisions for us, so many of which are accessible through prayer.

LIBERATION THROUGH CONFESSION

Mighty Jericho had fallen with a shout (Joshua 6:20) but now a far less formidable adversary, the city of Ai, put Israel's troops to rout. A distraught commander lay prostrate before Yahweh, looking to Him for the return of His favour. Joshua wasn't expecting what followed: 'Stand up!' said the LORD. 'What are you doing on your face? Israel has sinned ...' (Joshua 7:10-11a).

Sin had to be confessed before God's people could experience His blessings anew and move on in a positive direction. We, too, need to deal with our offences by confessing and turning from them if we sincerely desire God's richest blessings.

Norman Vincent Peale tells of a time in his boyhood when he tried to hide in an alley and feel grown up by smoking a big, black cigar. When his father appeared unexpectedly, Norman tried to snuff out the cigar while calling his dad's attention to a wall poster announcing the coming of the circus. With great buoyancy he pointed to the advertisement and asked if his dad would take him to the big top. He never forgot his father's response: 'Norman, never make a petition while holding on to a smouldering disobedience.'

It's imperative that we keep short accounts with God; 'He who conceals his sins does not prosper, but whoever confesses and renounces them finds mercy' (Proverbs 28:13). My tendency in confessing either sinful thoughts or deeds is to want to plead 'extenuating circumstances'. 'I'm sorry God, but so and so has been so unkind to me...' 'Forgive me, Father, but my desperate situation led me to...' When we come to God with these kinds of prefaces we're really seeking to justify ourselves; we're saying we only need a little bit of mercy, a smattering of grace; we're not all that bad and would have done better if our circumstances were more amenable to our needs.

Cries of self-justification are as old as Eden and are as valueless today as they were in the primeval garden. This shouldn't surprise us; none of us wants to acknowledge total responsibility for his evil acts. Yet if someone had offended you, to what kind of petition would you respond most readily, one which was couched in excuses or one which simply confessed wrong-doing and asked for forgiveness?

The latter approach is not only the most liberating as we seek to relate humbly to one another but also the only legitimate way to find full restoration with the holy God whose laws we continually flout. In this regard, we can learn much from David's petition following his sin with Bathsheba (Psalm 51:1-4); he offers no defence but simply pleads for mercy.

And God's mercy comes to us unstintingly each day, even as often as 'seventy times seven' (Matthew 18:22).

CRUCIAL CAVEAT

Remembering that Jesus taught us to pray 'forgive us as we forgive others' should put us in touch with His warning that if we withhold forgiveness from others, our Father will also withhold forgiveness from us (Matthew 6:14-15). Where would we be without His forgiveness? All access denied, we'd have to totally fend for ourselves. It's no wonder that Jesus told us to earnestly seek to be reconciled to those who have something against us and to even leave our place of worship in order for a resolution of our personal conflict to be found (Matthew 5:23-24). If we're nurturing a bitter, unforgiving spirit, we might as well not pray unless we first ask God for the grace to deal with it in the light of His Word.

WHAT, THEN, SHALL I SAY?

Our prayers for forgiveness should be open and honest before God. They should also be specific in response to the Holy Spirit's promptings, clearly stating the offence. We must remember how eagerly the Father anticipates our return (Luke 15:20) even when our motivation may be less than noble. (Recall how the prodigal son's repentance actually began in his stomach [Luke 15:16-18]). Ask Him for the grace to change and then accept His forgiveness; don't allow those forgiven sins to weigh heavily upon your heart any more.

For many generations the people of Israel took the promise of Micah quite literally when he said that Yahweh would 'hurl all their iniquities into the depths of the sea' (7:19). They could be found at the Jordan's banks ceremonially washing their iniquities into the depths of the river and, by faith, accepting God's thorough cleansing. Elsewhere God has promised to remove our sins from us 'as far as the east is from the west' (Psalm 103:12)—distancing us infinitely from them. Adopt the mindset of Paul who refused to dwell in the past, whose wide vision of God's forgiveness in Christ constrained him to focus only upon the glorious future (Philippians 3:13-14).

GRACE UNTO REPENTANCE

It was midnight when the phone rang. Friends of mine told me about a young man, a musician, who had recently returned from

California where he had been an instrumentalist with the San Francisco Symphony Orchestra. Once a member of the church, he left and pursued a homosexual lifestyle, eventually contracting AIDS. He was in an upstairs bedroom, dying. He had come home to die in the company of any who were willing to receive him. They asked if I'd come over and minister to him in whatever way I could.

I said I'd pray for him and would be glad to stop by early in the morning in response to their request. They weren't sure he would last that long but, owing to the lateness of the hour, refrained from pressing me to come.

As I set the phone down, desiring to get back to sleep, I prayed for Richard, that God would be merciful to him and draw him to the Saviour. I tried to relax but couldn't. The Holy Spirit wouldn't let me. It became increasingly evident that it was God's intention for me to go to Richard's bedside and pray there, not effortlessly from my supine position.

Hurriedly throwing on some clothes I quickly drove the few miles to my friends' house and proceeded to Richard's bedside. His breathing was laboured, his eyes unfocused. I took his skeletal hand in mine and began praying, this time with a sense of the presence of God. I don't remember the content of my prayer but I recall leaning close to him and singing: 'Jesus loves me, this I know; for the Bible tells me so . . .'. When I finished, an unearthly sense of peace filled my soul; I knew that the message of Christ's love had gotten through to him; that, by the grace of God, the reality of God's forgiving love had claimed Richard's heart.

My phone rang again early in the morning, this time to tell me that Richard had been called home; he was no longer a prodigal in the far country.

I learned a lesson that sometimes where you pray is as important as what you pray; that to be sensitive to the Holy Spirit's direction involves more than a desire to have Him pray through you. When unreality creeps into my prayer life I dare not overlook the question, 'Am I where He wants me to be?'

God's Word comes to us again and again, battering down our resistant walls (Jonah 3:1).

Upon listening to a sermon of George Whitefield, a Connecticut farmer wrote in his diary, 'My hearing him preach gave me a heart wound and by God's blessing ... my old foundation was broken up and I saw my righteousness would not save me.' God's wondrous work of making us aware of our need of His mercy and grace moved a Puritan to pray, '...wound my heart that it may be healed; break it that Thine own hand may make it whole.'

The spirit of these words connect well with those of David's: 'See if there is any offensive way in me, and lead me in the way everlasting' (Psalm 139:24). Like the psalmist we should ask God to make us aware of matters in our lives which cry out for His help to change.

Self-reformation, itself, will never do; the old nature will never release me to accomplish the radical change desired. No one understood our dilemma better than Paul when he said, 'I am unspiritual, sold as a slave to sin' (Romans 7:14). John Donne insightfully wrote of our plight, and offered a fitting plea:

> I, like a usurped town to another due,
> Labour to admit You, but oh! to no end;
> Reason, Your viceroy in me, me should defend,
> But it captived and proves weak or untrue.
> Yet dearly I love You, and would be loved fain,
> But am betrothed unto Your enemy.

Divorce me, untie, or break that knot again,
Take me to You, imprison me, For I
Except You enthral me, never shall be free;
Nor ever chaste, except You ravish me.

Although maudlin self-reflection is surely counter-productive—let's not be archaeologists digging up our remote past—there is value in asking God to make you conscious of offences which can then be confessed, turned from, and forgiven. In the process you may find this to be the means whereby your prayer life is revitalized and deepened.

7

Thankful Always

My wife and I were at table with a close relative who had just prepared a sumptuous dinner for us. Hoping to use this as an occasion to bring God into the picture I said to our host, 'You know, this is such a splendid feast, I'd like to offer thanks.' Our host's response quickly took the wind out of my sails: 'O, that's O.K., Stuart; I was glad to do it.'

Thanklessness towards God is a mark of pagan society (Romans 1:21); it is characteristic of humanism (which is nothing more than an inverted thanksgiving). As history moves to its stunning climax, gratitude will have noticeably diminished (2 Timothy 3:2).

Yet I am woefully irregular in communicating to God in a spirit of thankfulness; words which express my appreciation for who God is and what He has done for me are pretty sparse. If I were more thankful it would be less difficult for me to pray as I ought, for who could deny that coming to God with a grateful heart is both fundamental to, and enriches, genuine worship? Thomas Watson, a seventeenth century Puritan, observed that 'many have tears in their eyes, and complaints in their mouths, but few have harps in their hands, blessing and glorifying God'.

All the festivals of Israel were designed to jog my peoples' memory respecting Yahweh's redemptive acts on their behalf, that they might be thankful as they recall all His many benefits (Psalm 103:2). Moses warned Israel about the danger of spiritual amnesia, of becoming self-satisfied and forgetful once they were settled in Canaan; the consequence would be devastating (Deuteronomy 8:1-20).

We are disturbingly like the people of Israel: we've received so much from God but acknowledged so little. The psalmist levels this indictment against the people of God's choosing: 'But they soon forgot what He had done and did not wait for His counsel... they gave into their craving...' (Psalm 106:13-14).

In the traditional Passover service we sing an old Hebrew text whose chorus is earmarked by the word, *Dayenu*. Each stanza recounts some of the many things Yahweh has done for us as a people, such as giving us the manna, the law, the prophets, the Temple, and after each of them is mentioned, the word *Dayenu*, which exclaims that that blessing would have been sufficient all by itself and deserves praise, is repeated.

But the traditional Hebrew service doesn't go far enough in recognizing that our chief reason for thanks should be the privilege of entering into a personal relationship with God. Israel, of course, has yet to see how their Messiah has opened up the way for such intimacy with Yahweh.

Unfortunately, there are multitudes of Christians who either forget or take for granted what God has made available to them in Christ. It's nothing new; the ancient church had the very same tendency (Matthew 16:9-10; Revelation 3:3). Their forgetfulness is not so much an absent-mindedness as it is a failure to consciously savour the reality that God is truly present with them; He has even condescended to indwell them with His

Spirit. That in itself should prompt the cry, '*Dayenu*!'; but God has also seen to providing us with much, much more, including the little non-essentials which bring delight to our hearts.

Somewhere in a story of Sherlock Holmes, called *The Adventure of the Naval Treaty*, Dr. Watson observes Holmes as he holds up a moss rose, studying its extraordinary blend of crimson and green, whereupon he speaks, 'There is nothing in which deduction is so necessary as in religion ... Our highest assurance of the goodness of Providence seems to rest in the flowers ... This rose is an extra: its smell and its colour are an embellishment of life, and not necessary for our existence. It is only goodness which gives extras... '.

Recently I asked the members of a Bible class to daily record three distinctly different things for which they could give thanks to God. I found myself being thankful for some things I've long taken for granted, like a good cup of tea. And I was grateful that God had caused me to be born after tea was 'invented' (not to mention Danish pastry).

It's so easy to overlook the little things as well as the big ones, and to fail to be thankful. Do we have eyes but see not and ears but hear not? Has our sensitivity to His presence been somehow blunted? Disallowing any tendencies towards pantheism, even poetry may incite our thankfulness:

> Earth's crammed with heaven,
> And every common bush afire with God;
> But only he who sees who takes off his shoes —
> The rest sit round it and pluck blackberries.
>
> Elizabeth Barrett Browning

One of the happiest Christians I've ever known was a tall, wiry black man by the name of Luke, whom I met while visiting missionaries in impoverished north-western Haiti. He asked me to walk about with him so he could show me the wonderful things that God had done for him.

First he told me how grateful he was that God had given him a wife to love and to be loved by in return. Then we walked up a crude path to what was little more than a hut, less than the size of my living room back home. Words of joyful thanks filled the air as he recounted how his Jesus had made it possible for him to have such a splendid roof over his head. We walked a bit further and he pointed to a lean-to which he had built to provide shade and protection for those suffering from malaria. Again, a note of joy was sounded as he thanked God who had given him the strength and skill to bring that blessed provision to his homeless neighbours.

As the trail widened we came upon a cemetery where Luke paused to observe several of the grave markers. 'Some of my people are there,' he said. His speech became animated as he continued, gesturing skywards with his large hands. 'They are all going to rise, you know—RISE, one day!' In the hour or so that I spent with Luke I sensed I was in the presence of one who thoroughly knew what the Bible meant by the word 'Hallelu-YAH' (You praise the Lord!).

By recounting in detail some of the things the Lord had done for him, Luke was giving thanks to his heavenly Father. From his countenance it was evident that joy was linked to these expressions of gratitude. My Haitian brother found pleasure in speaking of the evidences of God's grace and doubtless brought joy to the heart of His unseen Benefactor as well.

There's a nearby healthcare facility for the handicapped where my wife has ministered as an R.N. for many years. It's truly refreshing to hear someone praise God for a new wheelchair or for the ability to take a few steps or read a few words. In a world which continuously gives man the credit for everything there are still those who are able to discern the real source for each and every one of life's blessings and respond thankfully to Him. Perhaps because of their extensive restrictions most of them have come to recognize how dependent they are upon God for everything.

As a pianist I recall the uplifting experience of accompanying two of the older residents who delighted in praising God through their favourite songs: *Because He lives I can face tomorrow* and *You gave me love when no one gave me a prayer*.

Our Father always delights in hearing His children speak thankfully concerning the blessings they've received from His hands. Perhaps you need to ask Him to give you an enlarged sensitivity to the innumerable things for which you should express your gratitude to Him. When asked how I'm doing I often answer, 'Better than I deserve.' It's not a facetious response; God owes me nothing. The only thing that is rightfully mine is His judgment; even the least of His blessings is by no means due me.

REJOICE ALWAYS?

Paul tells the Philippians to rejoice always (4:4) and immediately repeats it to stress its importance. We are told to be thankful in all circumstances; it's God's will for us (1 Thessalonians 5:18).

Is it always possible for you to be thankful? Jacob was essentially a man of faith yet we listen to his false conclusion that everything had turned against him (Genesis 42:36). Godly Naomi says, 'I went away full, but the Lord has brought me back empty ... the Almighty has brought misfortune upon me' (Ruth 1:21). These are not the words of joyful hearts.

It may seem strange to some, but I'm grateful for their presence in the Bible. I'm glad to read the psalmist's troubling thoughts (Psalm 55:2) and hear his perplexed cries (Psalm 10:1; 22:1). For it seems to me that when we express our deepest thoughts to God—even the sorrow-ridden disquieting ones—we open ourselves to receive His comfort and strength. It's important, therefore, to realise that we are in the presence of God when we vent our unhinged emotions. Furthermore we bring honour to God when we pour our hearts out before Him.

Whenever my children would come to me to tell me of some personal distress or problem I felt that they were, in a very special way, bringing their praise to me. By entrusting me with their thoughts they were, in effect, acknowledging me to be a good and caring father. When we speak openly before our incomparably good heavenly Father we are likewise bringing Him our praise.

As a young man I found it difficult to share my burdens with my father because he did not hear well and, because hearing aids were rather large in those days, he refused to even consider wearing one. By way of contrast, God is attentive to all that we think and say. Soren Kierkegaard, melancholy through his many afflictions, nonetheless reflected on God's care as he prayed: 'Thou art moved and moved in infinite love by all things: the need of a sparrow, even this moves Thee; and what we scarcely see, a human sigh, this moves Thee, O infinite Love!'

Even our tears are precious to Him (Psalm 56:8); the binding up of our wounds takes precedence over His concern for the galaxies (Psalm 147:2-4). In view of that, Dr. Paul Tournier counselled his patients who found it hard to pray, 'Talk to God as you are talking to me; even more simply, in fact.'

SEEING THE UNSEEN

I'm convinced that, like Jacob when he said 'everything's against me,' we often speak out of our ignorance. Because we are finite, fallen creatures, our vantage point will always be characterized by partial knowledge and limited insight. Notwithstanding Jacob's suppositions, the objective truth remained: God had been working all things together for Jacob's good, as He has on behalf of each of His people throughout all generations (Romans 8:28). And because He has promised never to forsake us (Matthew 28:20; Hebrews 13:5) His Holy Spirit ultimately revives us with the truth that He really does love us which, in turn, gives rise to a renewed thankfulness.

In 1636 during the Thirty Years' War, a German pastor, Martin Rinkart, is said to have buried five thousand of his parishioners—an average of fourteen a day. In the midst of that period of horrible devastation he wrote this table grace for his children, one of my favourite hymns:

> Now thank we all our God
> With hearts and hands and voices;
> Who wondrous things hath done,
> In whom His world rejoices.
> Who, from our mother's arms
> hath led us on our way
> With countless gifts of love
> And still is ours today.

Rinkart knew something about the love of God which we also need to know: it is constant and completely independent of circumstances. That all-conquering love has come to absorb our grief and nullify death's terrifying power. Returning to an earlier statement from George MacDonald, 'Until God can wipe away all our tears' (Revelation 21:4)—an event which truly may be sooner than most of us imagine—'He would have them flow without bitterness; to which end He tells us that it is a blessed thing to mourn (Matthew 5:4), because of the comfort on its way.'

UNSPOKEN THANKS

There are several events in my life for which I have not been able to give God thanks—at least not vocally. In the depths of my heart I wonder how God will ever make all of those discordant experiences 'work together for good' (Romans 8:28). Yet I am thankful that He is in control, that not a molecule in this entire universe operates independently of His good and perfect will; thus the painful things which sometimes cloud my vision of His goodness are somehow part of His benevolent plan for my life.

Someday, I sense, that Holy Spirit-prompted inner conviction will express itself freely through my lips; until that day I believe the Holy Spirit is offering appropriately thankful words on my behalf. Doubtless, the conflicts, testings, and pressures are all part of His plan to enable me to develop, spiritually. It is good when we can receive His Fatherly discipline silently, without complaining (Hebrews 12:7); that, too, is acceptable to God, and worshipful.

8
A Place for Praise

Praise and thankfulness are bedfellows in that they are expressed by souls made aware of qualities which are uniquely found in God. The two are also bound together because the thankful prayer is invariably an expression of praise; similarly, the one who praises God is certainly manifesting a spirit of thankfulness.

An immediately discernable difference—at least in terms of their practice—is that our expression of thanks tends to be prompted by some personal experience of God's benevolence while praise is more often launched by an apprehension of such divine characteristics as His sovereignty, power, majesty, or grace.

The earliest prayer taught me at my synagogue was called the *Sh 'mah* (Hebrew for 'Hear!') which was simply an affirmation of the oneness of Yahweh found in Deuteronomy 6:4. In its entirety it comprised Deuteronomy 6:4-9; 11:13-21 and Numbers 15: 37-41. Our forebears coupled the initial sentence with an expression of praise proclaiming the eternal nature of God's kingdom. It must have been reasoned that, since God is one, there can ultimately be only one kingdom; and the fact of His sovereign rule should draw praise from all of His subjects. Several blessings accompanied the *Sh 'mah*; the earliest of them embellishes the truth of His incomparable greatness:

> Blessed art Thou, O Lord our God, King of the world,
> Former of light and Creator of darkness, Maker of peace and
> Creator of all things; Who gives light in mercy to the earth
> and to those who live thereon; And in His goodness renews
> every day, continually, the work of creation. Let a new light
> shine over Zion and Thy Messiah's light over us.

To say that God is the one and only ruler probably seems quite elementary to us—it wasn't all that remarkable to me when I first recited the *Sh'mah*. Yet to my ancient ancestors it came as a profound revelation, given them to embrace and proclaim against a thoroughly polytheistic culture.

Like them we need to be moved by the awesome wonder generated by the fact of God's oneness; *Sh'mah!* means to hear deeply—to fully embrace that which is being said. We may not be as wretched as the Narnia Chronicles' Eustus whose hardness stands in need of the lion Aslan's radical 'surgery'; we may simply have grown stale on the truth and need to step back to reconsider this foundation again, as it were, through the wonderment of a little child's gaze. (To this end, recall Jesus' indignant rebuke in Mark 10:15.)

Open your heart afresh to consider the implications of what has been revealed to us: if there is one God there is only one way, one revelation, one power and ultimate reality—one Rock upon whom we place our hope and seek to build our lives. Here's a truly wonderful motivation to praise God: He has taken so much of the guesswork and uncertainty out of life.

In addition to delighting in 'that great original simplicity of a single authority in all things,' G. K. Chesterton reviews history's many religious traditions and contrasts them all with Christ whom He calls 'the enormous exception'. In the Preface to his book, *The Eternal Man*, he says "The most that any primitive myth had ever suggested was that the Creator was present at the Creation. But that the Creator was present ... in the daily life of the Roman Empire—that is something utterly unlike anything else in nature. It is the one great startling statement that man has made since he spoke his first articulate word ... it makes nothing but dust and nonsense of comparative religion.' Pause once again to reflect upon the miracle of this one God revealing Himself personally to us, condescending, as He did, to walk among us— and covenanting within Himself to do so long before anyone had a prayer.

We will find it hard to repress our praise whenever we deeply consider the overarching purpose for His becoming one of us. None states the reason more forcefully than the apostle John: 'This is how God showed His love among us: He sent His one and only Son into the world that we might live through Him' (1 John 4:9). Praise generated by this truth can only become even more animated when we read John's following enlargement upon the revealed great news: 'This is love: not that we loved God, but that He loved us and sent His Son as an atoning sacrifice for our sins' (v.10).

But the wonder of His love doesn't end there; He died for us to make us sons in His very own family. 'Look at this lavish love,' John tells the church (1 John 3:1); behold the incredible love which has actually made us God's children. Our sonship was the great goal of Jesus Christ's coming (Romans 8:29; Galatians 4:4-7). As we ponder the boundless love of the Father we will increasingly find ourselves attending to the primary purpose of prayer: offering Him praiseful worship.

My studies in the synagogue taught me many things about Yahweh; but never did I learn to call Him 'Father'. Perhaps that's why the prayers of our traditional prayer book—the prayers of the fathers—failed to incite me to worship. In the many years I participated in the worship of my synagogue the closest I came to appreciating His paternalism was in the context of reading of the collective sonship of Israel (as noted, for example, in Exodus 4:22). Nowhere in our vast history was it ever typical for an Israelite to cry '*Abba*, Father' (Romans 8:15; Galatians 4:6). In the 'Eighteen Benedictions' which, from antiquity, have been an integral part of our synagogue worship, 'our Father' (*abinu*) occurs in the fourth and sixth of them; in neither instance, however, does the prayer lead the worshipper to think of himself as a child addressing his Father in the way that Jesus' disciples are oriented in their simple Aramaic utterance, *abba* (Luke 11:2).

MORE HELP FROM THE PAST

A collection of prayers from our Puritan fathers reveal a deep insight into the kind of devotion which characterized their drawing near to God. It's tremendously worthwhile to note the way their prayers began, how they addressed God—especially, their spiritually-sensitive diversity: 'O Supreme Moving Cause', 'O Fountain of all good', 'O Lover to the uttermost', 'Thou Blessed Spirit, Author of all grace and comfort', 'O God of my Exodus', 'Incomprehensible, great, and glorious God', 'Sovereign Commander of the universe', 'O Love beyond compare', 'O Lover of the loveless'. These are just a sampling of opening words which helped mould and contribute to an enriched and satisfying prayer life.

One of the great appeals of the charismatic movement is its

offering a diversified vocabulary—tongues—to those who sense an inadequacy in their worship and desire a greater fluency in praising God. How marvellous to be able to praise God without restraint--to be carried along unfettered by the one Moses called *Ruach Elohim* (Genesis 1:2).

For the Puritans, the variety expressed in their prayers was prompted by the Scriptures, themselves. In the Appendix to his book, *Pray With Your Eyes Open*, Dr. Richard Pratt lists hundreds of names, titles, and metaphors for God which are discoverable through spending time in God's Word. In studying the Scriptures we will continue to grow in our knowledge of God and learn to address Him in a host of diverse, enriching ways.

But it's essential to realize that God is not really concerned with the richness of our vocabulary or how we turn a phrase or if our sentence structure is grammatically correct. My wife has often prayed with a handicapped young man who loves the Lord but, because of a childhood injury, is unable to articulate even the simplest word. Although Brian's strange sounds seem unintelligible, they are nonetheless meaningful to God for they come from a heart touched by, and dependent upon, His love.

FROM PRAISE TO PETITION

Author Derek Prime, in *Created to Praise*, shows that when praise focuses on the attributes of God it serves as a mighty spur to seeking His help for our many needs and crises. Take for example the experience of the persecuted church in Acts 4. When the believers were threatened and ordered to stop speaking about Jesus they immediately brought the matter to God in prayer. Their starting point was Yahweh's almighty power:

'Sovereign Lord,' they said, 'You made the heaven and the earth and the sea, and everything in them' (4:24).

Their praise moves from the acknowledgement of the fact of one God on the throne of the universe to the remembrance of His having spoken authoritatively in the second Psalm about the patent foolishness of striving to stand against Him. It is clear that their subsequent petition for His help—for boldness in speech and accompanying miracles— rises out of whom they know God to be and what they know God to have said. Out of that realization they ask God to work mightily, not asking Him to remove the obstacles but to give grace commensurate with their need. And God does, filling them with His Holy Spirit in a powerful, demonstrative way (4:31).

At least two essentials are discernable in the drama recorded in Acts 4: first, the believers set their attention on God rather than on their difficulties; second, they begin with praise as they focus upon His qualities and promises. Nor is this the only time that this kind of reaction occurs in the lives of those undergoing great trials. Consider the cruel treatment of Paul and Silas, severely beaten and imprisoned at Philippi (Acts 16:23-24). Their hymn singing at midnight can only be seen as an expression of their praise for God and confidence in His ultimate deliverance. Instead of saying, 'O Lord, how are we ever going to make it through this crisis?' they begin with praising their faithful God whose Person and promises are altogether reliable.

Sometimes my situation seems so severe I'm forced to say, 'How can God *not* help!?' When problems began to overwhelm me last year I started a journal in which I recorded some of the ways God was providing for me and my family. As I look back upon those evidences of God's faithfulness I draw confidence as I face today's difficulties. Thus, through the witness of Scripture as well as my personal experiences of God's grace I am encouraged and am learning to praise Him irrespective of my circumstances.

He may be giving you more than you think you can bear to show the sufficiency of His grace (2 Corinthians 1:8-9). Regardless of your plight, the power of God is always more than adequate to bring you through (1 Corinthians 10:13). Despite our inconsistencies and failures He does not change and will never forsake the work of His hands (Psalm 138:8; Hebrews 13:5). We must try to remember one thing: He is always at hand; 'in Him we live and move and have our being' (Acts 17:28).

Speaking from the 73rd Psalm, Dr. Martyn Lloyd-Jones encouraged his people with these words: 'Whatever may be happening around us, whatever may be happening inside us, we can go to the One who is always the same, the same in His might, His majesty, His glory, His love, His mercy, His compassion, and the same in all that He has promised ... Let us think more about God. Let us turn our minds and hearts towards Him. Let us realize that in Christ He offers us His fellowship, His companionship, and that constantly and always.'

9
Vital Specifics

Whenever we want help to pray we need to remember that the Bible is a veritable treasury of resources. We do well regularly to consult the Psalms for direction, even using them *verbatim* as the vehicle for our worship. We may say brief sections of a Psalm, embellishing it with thoughts triggered by the words we've read; or we may study a Psalm and allow God's revelation to mould and stimulate our own devotional response. As we become more familiar with the Psaltery we'll learn where to turn for inspiration when certain situations confront us.

In addition, the Scriptures are replete with many prayers of godly men and women, all of them granting us insight respecting how we should pray. You'll never outgrow your need to learn from their experiences. Note, for example, how Israel's premier statesman, Daniel, prayed on the basis of what he'd learned as he studied the prophecy of Jeremiah (Daniel 9:2-4).

It is evident that our Lord taught His disciples His well-known model prayer with the understanding that its several components, which encompass a host of essential matters, would serve well to guide their devotional lives. Luke records Jesus' response to a disciple's request for guidance in prayer with the words, 'When you pray, say' (Luke 11:2), showing that the instructive prayer was appropriate to use just as it was given. Matthew, however, tells us that Jesus told His disciples to 'pray then like this' (6:9), indicating that the prayer was to serve as a model to inform and inspire their own prayers.

Carefully studying the prayer in detail should prove to be a profitable exercise in helping us strike a balance in our worship by beginning with God—our Father whose glorious reign must increase through embracing His will—rather than with ourselves and our desires. In saying 'The Lord's Prayer' it's so easy to lose sight of what should be our primary concern: that God's Name be 'hallowed'—regarded as holy—by His creatures. This petition includes more than the way people speak about God; it is concerned with mankind's overall attitude and personal response to Him—that they would truly reverence Him.

As we come to that place where we're concerned for God's greater glory rather than just our own needs, we'll want to seek direction for our prayers from Jesus' intercession for the church in John 17. There we'll read of His concerns for His flock and what He asks His heavenly Father to do on their behalf. How often do we think to pray for the things which Jesus views as priorities? Give yourself to the study of verses 6-26 and ask the Holy Spirit to enable you to see the petitions which should legitimately serve as guidelines for your own words of intercession.

In keeping with this thought let's consider how we may better pray for others—in particular, members of the family of God. If there's an overworked expression in our prayer vocabulary it's surely the word 'bless'. 'O Lord,' we pray, 'Bless my dear brother (or sister) so and so.' Perhaps we'll include the adverb 'mightily' to add a bit more substance to our plea; notwithstanding, the vagueness of the prayer remains. What do we mean by 'bless'?

DISCERNING HIS PURPOSE TO BLESS

God really does want to bless His people. For me, as a boy, the most dynamic moment in the synagogue's worship service was the point in time when the rabbi, with uplifted hands, pronounced Yahweh's ancient benediction on His covenant people: 'Yevorechechah Adonai v'yishmorechah...' (The Lord bless thee and keep thee)... began the Aaronic line (Numbers 6:24-26). In this way, the Lord told Moses, the priests were to place the Name of God on His people for their blessing (Numbers 6:27). To have the light of God's Face shine upon you was seen as the best, not to mention the most essential, of all possible blessings.

Slightly to the right of the Sacred Scrolls in the front of the very old synagogue where I worshipped there hung a shining globe with a tiny bright light at its core. We called this 'The Eternal Light' and its purpose was to remind us of the glorious *Shekinah* (from the Hebrew word 'to dwell'). As a child I used to stare at the bright inner light and wonder about its source. I recall how distressed I was that one Sabbath when the light was extinguished—someone had inadvertently shut off the oil supply that kept it lit—and might have, had I been better informed, cried 'Ichabod!'

Irrespective of the absence of helpful symbols, God has purposed to bless His children by placing His powerful Name upon them—to place the light of His Face upon them; it's at the very core of the new covenant promise (Jeremiah 31:34; Ezekiel 36:27). So when we pray for others we should keep to the forefront what God's goal is for His own.

PRAYING WITH PAUL

It is with profound sensitivity to the full implications of God's immutable promise that Paul prays for the church:

> I pray that out of His glorious riches He may strengthen you with power through His Spirit in your inner being, so that Christ may dwell in your hearts through faith. And I pray that you, being rooted and established in love, may have power, together with all the saints, to grasp how wide and long and high and deep is the love of Christ, and to know this love that surpasses knowledge—that you may be filled to the measure of the fullness of God" (Ephesians 3:16-19).

Quite a prayer! And quite specific in terms of the content of God's blessing. It is integrally related to Paul's earlier, ongoing prayer for the church, in which he asks 'the glorious Father' to enable the Ephesians to know the hope that lies ahead of them, their extraordinary inheritance, and the 'incomparably great power' available to them through faith (Ephesians 1:17-19). All this is preceded by the apostle's offering up thanks for these people for whom he prays (v.16) and informs us that, as we pray for others, we also ought to begin by thanking God for them (even the ones whom we may find to be unpleasant).

First, Paul asks God to make His people aware of the hope to which they've been called. The hope is not some vague expectation but, rather, a certainty in Christ and an assured prospect.

As a boy I often enjoyed watching one of the earliest T.V. personalities, Arthur Godfrey, who hosted a daytime variety show. He would often read advertisements as a part of his comic routine and then comment on them. Once he read these words from a magazine: 'At last there's hope for middle age,' and then, turning to the camera, exclaimed: 'Hope! I *have* hope; what I need is *help!*'

For the Ephesians, God's hope abounded with help, for it was the Holy Spirit who was living in them guaranteeing their future (v.14). When we pray for others we need to ask God to encourage them—especially in the midst of crises—with a growing awareness of what God has in store for them, plans to wonderfully prosper them (Jeremiah 29:11).

Next, Paul asks that God would increasingly help them realize the riches of their inheritance among (NIV='in') the saints. Since it is within the sphere of Christian fellowship that we deepen in our understanding of what God has laid up in store for us, we ought never to forsake that precious communion (Hebrews 10:25).

Upsetting experiences cause many people to cut themselves off from others; instead of reaching out for support they withdraw from others. In doing so they cut themselves off from the means of their encouragement—their spiritual revitalization. During traumatic times nothing has helped me more than the prayers of those in the church who've petitioned the Father on my behalf.

In my Jewish tradition a duly-constituted prayer meeting requires the presence of at least ten men. Called a *minyan* (quorum), it recognizes the power of intercession—what God will do 'for the sake of ten ...' (Genesis 18:32). Hardly anything is more encouraging that the realization that others are seeking God's help on your behalf.

Ever since one of my sons moved to a city where there is a scant Christian witness I've been praying that God will lead him to a church where he will be encouraged and built up in the things of the Lord. It is appropriate to pray that believers will seek and find the kind of fellowship which will enhance their understanding of what ultimately awaits them (Isaiah 64:4; 1 Corinthians 2:9), a reward which is, in reality, God Himself (Genesis 15:1; 1 John 3:2). As this promised future grips our hearts and minds more fully, the result will be a life brought into closer conformity with the will of God (1 John 3:3). That, in turn, cannot but exert a positive influence on all that we think and pray.

Finally, the apostle asks that the church may know 'the immeasurable greatness of His power' (Ephesians 1:19). Paul wants us to experience the kind of incredible power that raised Christ from the dead and seated Him in the heavenly realms (v.20). As God's fathomless power was manifested in His Son, so its vital expression is to be seen in the lives of all who trust in Christ; it is the power of God the Holy Spirit for which we are encouraged to pray (cf. Luke 11:13).

This prayer is immensely practical because virtually all of life's problems and challenges have a spiritual root. 'Unreality in religion,' J. I. Packer points out in *Knowing God*, 'is an accursed thing.' Conversely, meeting life's problems and opportunities with a true perception of reality is a blessed thing, making all the difference in whether or not we handle them successfully. If we really know that we are passionately loved by God (cf. Hosea for enthralling insight), that His plans for us are good, and that great internal power—the power of God Himself—is available to us through faith, we will not only emerge unscathed from the assaults of life but also find our prayers less preoccupied with paltry matters.

It is regrettably true that, although all Christians may say, according to Scripture, that the Holy Spirit indwells them (1 Corinthians 12:3), comparatively few live in such a way as to give credence to the doctrine that they are being supernaturally controlled. We live in a society which has been impregnated with Christianity but which has long ceased believing it and is really quite indifferent to the claims of Christ.

Those who do acknowledge Christ as Lord often manifest precious little which in any way marks them as new creations (2 Corinthians 5:17), set apart by God's life-transforming grace. The vast majority need the "eyes of their heart enlightened" (Ephesians 1:18); we need to pray this for them—and for ourselves. 'What am I the better,' John Owen reasons, 'if I can dispute that Christ is God but have no sense of sweetness in my heart from hence that He is a God in covenant with my soul?'

What hangs in the balance is more than just our own personal growth and encouragement; it is the advance of the kingdom of God (for which, hopefully, we pray in accordance with Jesus' instructive prayer). To deepen in the apprehension of our vital present inheritance—'all things are yours' (1 Corinthians 3:21)—cannot help but have a salutary effect on the content and frequency of our prayers.

To say that we believe in the Holy Spirit—as, for example, we affirm in the Apostles' Creed —should mean that we have confidence in the presence of God to indwell us and apply the truth of His Word in life-changing ways. Epaphras, who wrestled in prayer with the hopes of seeing the believers at Colossae mature in their faith (Colossians 4:12), surely counted on a miracle-working God to do just that.

10
When You Shouldn't Have a Prayer

I've been at a prayer meeting where the minister looked out over the congregation and received a number of 'unspoken requests' from those gathered to pray. The communication ran something like this: 'Yes, brother, I see that hand'; 'Thank you, sister, for your request.' 'Over there in the corner—you have two unspoken requests?' This pattern having been repeated several times, the minister then prayed something like this: 'Father, you see these hands and know the petitions. We bring them to You and ask You to answer them in Jesus' Name. Amen.'

I'm sure they all meant well but it's hard to be too impressed (in a positive way) about this type of praying. Entering into that kind of scenario should be all but impossible for those who take the business of prayer seriously. At the very least it militates against truly bearing another's burdens (Galatians 6:2) and makes fervency virtually impossible (cf. Colossians 4:12).

There's a much more common situation which may ordinarily face us. A fellow pastor described it somewhat like this: you are earnestly asked to pray for Jim: he's out of work and cannot make his mortgage payments—he could even lose his home; what a terrible state of affairs! Then as you're about to begin praying for Jim you recall that, for as long as you've known him, he's never really contributed to the work of the church; nor has he used his residence in any way to reach out to the lost or to encourage the saints.

You might then ask yourself if Jim's loss of his job—and his house—are matters about which you really feel motivated to pray? Perhaps the Lord is not all that concerned about the prosperity of someone who's lived pretty much for himself all these years. Could it be that the Lord is using these unpleasant experiences to help Jim get his priorities straight? Furthermore, are you concerned enough regarding Jim's plight that you're willing to do anything you can to help him through this rough period? If you personally have resources but are unwilling to make them available to Jim, will the prayer you make on his behalf be acceptable to God? (See James 2:15-17.)

I was at another worship service where a young lady asked us to pray that God would provide her with funds necessary to journey overseas for a brief season of ministry. The pastor asked me to lead in prayer. As I began I made mention of the fact that the Lord knew where the needed finances were to be found and that He who owned the cattle on a thousand hills could easily tap those resources on behalf of my needy sister. I was in the middle of a sentence when it was as if God said to me, 'Stuart, you have enough money to cover her expenses; you pay her way.' So I interrupted myself and abruptly ended what could have been an unnecessarily extended petition.

There may be a number of intercessors who need to consider the possibility that they, themselves, have the ability to meet the needs of those for whom they pray. If we're unwilling to consider the role God may want us to play in answering the requests of others we need to understand more fully what it means to be a vital member of the body of Christ.

'IF IT BE YOUR WILL'

Since Jesus' request to be spared from the cross was accompanied by these words, many seem to believe that this phrase should be added to virtually every supplication they make. They are reluctant to simply lay their petition before their Father. I've often observed this when God is called upon to help someone in desperate straights: 'O Lord, You are the great Physician; whenever you touched the diseased they were made whole. Now Mary is ill and the doctors don't know if she'll pull through. But she's Your child, Lord, and You're able to restore her; raise her up to health again ... if it is Your will.'

Every child of God should come to Him with a humble, submissive attitude. We should never lose sight of His sovereign right to answer any of our requests—even those which seem rightly motivated and desirous of His glory—with a 'No'. If we proceed to pray with this settled understanding, there's no compelling reason for the appendage, 'If it be Your will,' when we bring our petition to the Father. I've always thought it best to reserve that expression for those times when I really don't have the vaguest notion what the will of God is in a given situation.

Whenever possible, we ought to be as specific as possible in our requests and, as implied earlier, avoid asking for undefined 'blessings' on behalf of others. It is one thing to be specific; another thing to be unnecessarily wordy. I've been at prayer gatherings where, to hear the amount of detail offered—'Here we are, Lord, at Village Bible Church in the heart of Nebraska at noonday'—, you'd think God needed to be informed as if He were a visiting stranger. He knows your Zip code and all of the details of your life; you can get to the point without all the verbiage.

NAME IT AND CLAIM IT?

If my child has an 105° fever it makes little sense for me to pray, 'God, Your Word tells me no harm will befall me, no disaster come near my dwelling' (Psalm 91:10). While there may be, as someone has said, 30,000 promises in the Bible, not all of them are mine all of the time. In the case of my fever-stricken son it would appear more appropriate—and honest—to quote from such a text as Isaiah 43:1-2 where God promises to be with His people in their trials and support them in even the most vexing situations. One thing is evident: unless the Holy Spirit quickens a particular verse to my heart I am ill-advised to simply choose any verse I happen to fancy and indiscriminately attempt to apply it to my problem.

HELP OF THE HELPLESS

Few things have the potential for greater discouragement than what appear to be unanswered prayers, particularly those which have been repeatedly offered to God over a lengthy stretch of time. It could not have been all that easy for the church to pray zealously for the apostle Peter's release from prison upon receiving news of the execution of John's brother, James, by godless King Herod (See Acts 12:1-16). Notwithstanding, they would not allow disappointment to dissuade them from petitioning the Lord on behalf of Peter (albeit with little anticipation of the dramatic results described somewhat tongue-in-cheek).

I was ministering in Connecticut and visited with a recently married young woman whose husband had died from an inoperable brain tumour. Many had prayed for his healing, but to no avail; months of frustration had culminated in Steve's death. Judy had come to accept the loss of her husband as a part of God's perfect, yet mysterious will. Her hard experience had taught her something which she capsulized in the following manner: 'People will tell you "time heals", but it's not true; only Jesus heals.' In spite of what she had gone through, the Holy Spirit ultimately brought her that peace of heart she so desperately desired but which had been so terribly elusive.

Following his return to the pulpit after the sudden death of his wife, a Scottish preacher, Arthur Gossip, brought a message titled, 'When Life Tumbles In, What Then?' He told his congregation that although life was indeed a puzzle, more puzzling still was that individual who could abandon his faith in times of great personal loss. 'Abandon it for what?' he said. When life's dark events assault us His presence is the only light on an otherwise dreary path (see John 6:68).

O LORD, HOW LONG?

As a boy, while rummaging in the attic, I discovered a book written about the Messiah. In a dark place, covered with cobwebs, it had obviously been disposed of quite unceremoniously. I tried to understand it but the contents were too advanced for someone so young as I. It was evidently written by a former rabbi who had come to accept Jesus as his Messiah. Curiosity drove me back to it from time to time; I had never seen anything like it.

Many years later, after God's grace transformed my life, I thought again of that little dusty volume in that remote part of my house and reached this tentative conclusion: someone had been concerned enough for the souls of my family to give us a book with the hope that it might lead one or more of us to faith in the Saviour. It is also most likely that whoever gave the book would have prayed for its recipients, that God would open their hearts to receive His Son. I believe that the Lord ultimately used that person's prayers to draw me to the Messiah. The one who gave the book is probably completely unaware of what his prayers (could it have been just one prayer?) accomplished. We must not be discouraged when our prayers do not bring immediate results.

When do you stop asking? How long must you persevere? We know that, although the apostle Paul's request for healing was denied, the Lord made clear to Paul the reason for the denial and extended a very special grace to him to enable him to cope with his 'stake in the flesh' (2 Corinthians 12:7-9). Although our problems do provide us with opportunities to learn more about grace and dependence, not all will receive God's answer in the way described by Paul in the above passage; God deals with each of us as a unique individual.

Jesus told his disciples that they 'should always pray and not give up' (Luke 18:1). Yet is that imperative applicable to every one of life's situations? The accompanying parable in league with Jesus' statement centred on justice being administered on behalf of God's chosen ones who, like so many of the oppressed righteous, cry out day and night for heaven's vindication (Luke 18:7-8). Sometimes I'm quite reluctant to pray for justice; God might just give it to me!

More generally helpful may be Jesus' parable dealing with an appeal to a friend at midnight when there is inadequate bread to feed a visitor. We need never be ashamed to come to the Lord and keep on asking; He directs us to do so. Have you ever considered how differently things might have turned out if Elijah had discontinued praying with his sixth appeal for rain? (See 1 Kings 18:44).

Jesus says to ask, seek, and knock—and to do so continually with the assurance that God will 'give good gifts to those who ask' (Luke 11:13). The choicest response to our need, however, is the gift of the Holy Spirit for whom we are instructed to pray (v. 13). This was God's final consolation for the bereaved widow, Judy.

Only the Holy Spirit can cause us to see that our eternal destiny with Christ in heaven is not Plan B in case our lives are unhappy on planet Earth. Jesus wants us to focus upon that ultimate certainty of life with Him over against which everything we have to endure here will one day reveal its truly evanescent character. That person always has a prayer who has discarded his treasure maps of earth knowing that his priceless possessions dwell where moth and rust do not destroy (Matthew 6:19-21).

REMEMBERING THE REBELLIOUS

I've recently prayed with a young man whose wife walked out on him about two years ago. Suzie decided that she had had it with Bob; neither had she any more interest in Christianity. Since then Bob has been praying for Suzie to come back to him and renew her commitment both to him and to the Lord. Others have been praying to this end as well. How much longer should they all pray? Is the time coming for this unhappy situation to be viewed as final?

We know that God hates divorce (Malachi 2:16) and that He delights in reconciliation. Is that enough to enable a soul to persevere and 'never give up' (Luke 18:1)? There is no easy answer to this question. No one can decide this for Bob; he'll have to arrive at a workable conclusion for himself as he looks to God for guidance.

It's said that George Mueller prayed for more than fifty

years that one of his dearest friends would become a Christian.
His friend was converted—three months following Mueller's
death. Yet it cannot be denied that, in the words of commentator
George Adam Smith, 'love sometimes stands defeated on the
battlefield of life'. Perhaps the content of Bob's prayers for
Suzie will have to change someday if, for reasons perhaps
known only to the Lord, his wife refuses to return.

Somewhere in Paul Tournier's writings the insightful
counsellor tells of a friend who, contrary to Dr. Tournier's
advice and prayers, was planning to divorce his wife. Tournier
knew that, under God's guidance, a solution other than divorce
could be found. Yet the needs of his friend for the doctor's
support moved him to conclude, 'If he gets his divorce, he will
no doubt meet even greater difficulties than those he is in today.
He will need my affection all the more ...'.

Paul had determined to love his friend unreservedly, to
assure him of his unconditional commitment, to be true to his
covenant of friendship which was but a reflection of God's
covenantal faithfulness (1 John 4:19). We all have different
thresholds; it's ill-advised for anyone to view another critically
because he's unable to prayerfully persevere as we think he
ought. Nor could we be certain that we'd act any differently
than him if we were in his place.

Prayer might not come easily when we disagree with the
action of another; nonetheless, genuine love must not fail to
supplicate on behalf of a hurting brother. With this in mind we
should recall the words of one of Israel's greatest leaders,
Samuel, when he told his errant people, 'As for me, far be it
from me that I should sin against the Lord by failing to pray for
you' (1 Samuel 12:23). Why was Samuel moved to uphold a
recalcitrant nation in prayer? He clearly states his reasoning in

the previous verse: 'For the sake of His great Name the Lord will not reject His people, because the Lord was pleased to make you His own.'

No one articulated God's faithful covenant more passionately than the prophet, Hosea, whose faithless wife's departure was paralleled by the Hebrew people's abandonment of Yahweh. Contrary to those whose conception of God holds Him coolly detached from His people we hear Him cry out through Hosea: 'How can I give you up...? My heart is changed within Me; all My compassion is aroused' (Hosea 11:8). When we consider the depths of God's love for His children—even for such a wayward soul as me—we must be terribly hard-hearted to withhold our petitions on their behalf.

My rabbi taught that Judaism did not expect us to love our enemies but neither did its tenets permit us to deny them help if they were in need. He could not understand, however, how Jesus could actually expect anyone to love and pray for his adversaries (Matthew 5:44). Enemies were people for whom you shouldn't have a prayer (although twelfth among the so-called Eighteen Benedictions of ancient Judaism prayed that Christians would 'perish as in a moment').

Jesus obviously expects a great deal from His disciples, things which would be impossible were it not for two interconnected truths: first, we have been made new—born from above—by His Spirit who has enabled us to personally encounter the living God as our very own Father; second, the same Holy Spirit is at work in our lives empowering us to put into practice the kind of love Jesus has made known to us.

There's an unassailable inner logic to it all: Christ loved us when we were yet His enemies and commands us to follow His example; Christ gives to us the same Holy Spirit whose anointing animated His ministry in order that we might obey Him. So grace begets grace: grace to think, to act, and to pray.

I'm amazed when I learn that the primitive church prayed for a brute like Nero; my emotions say I shouldn't have a prayer for him (unless it's like the Jews' prayer for the Czar in *Fiddler on the Roof* asking God to distance him from me). Apparently they took the teaching of Scripture seriously (1 Timothy 2:1-2); so must I!

11

A Prayerful Song

In my synagogue, singing was not frequently required of the congregation; the responsibility for leading the people to the Almighty in song was entrusted largely to the *chazan*, or cantor. After all, he had the really good voice and was, next to the rabbi, most fluent in Hebrew. Although we were familiar with many of the psalms, we seemed to have lost sight of the fact that they were originally sung, not spoken. (In the Hebrew Bible, the title of the Psalms, *T'hillim*, means 'Songs of Praise'.)

Singing is not an activity I do naturally; it is not something my temperament and gifts produce spontaneously. Aesthetically, I feel much more comfortable when I'm using piano chords rather than vocal chords. There are times, however, when acting contrary to my proclivities is definitely advantageous.

In the house of God, singing gives me the opportunity to lift my voice with others in corporate worship; it is a way to pray with my brothers and sisters. The purpose of worshipping in this manner is not, primarily, a means for me to experience some sort of emotional 'high'; it is because God is worthy to be praised in song; He has ordained music to be used to that end (Psalm 33:3; 40:3).

For the event to achieve its purposes, however, I must make

the words as well as the music mine. John Wesley would often stop his people in the midst of a congregational hymn and say, 'Now! do you know what you said last? Did you speak no more than you felt? Did you sing it as unto the Lord; with the Spirit and with the understanding also?' Like many other spiritual leaders, the Wesleys knew that well-written hymns could provide the worshipper with a Bible commentary, a devotional guide, and a resource for prayer all in one. Immerse yourself in the great hymns of a Watts or a Wesley if you find yourself on the dry side; you'll be stimulated to worship as you realise with what a fine assortment of ready-made prayers you've been provided.

When it is hard for me to pray alone, joining with others of like precious faith definitely gives me 'a leg up'. In that context it is a far less formidable task for me to remember I'm singing to the Lord of the universe who condescendingly welcomes even the devoted shouts of children (Matthew 21:15-16).

In addition, the Scriptures give me the spectacular assurance that my adoration is being joined to that of the whole of God's elect in heaven—including the angels' (Hebrews 12:22-23). When such worship is from the heart it actually becomes what Dr. Edmund Clowney liked to call 'doxological evangelism', which means that our praiseful adoration draws others to the Lord and they're converted.

As a young Christian I often attended a service of worship which encouraged spontaneity in worshipful song. While the experience had an overall uplifting quality to it, a certain sameness tended to pervade the group's 'singing in the Spirit'; a three-part major chord hung perpetually on the air; and people who were basically non-musical sang non-musically. Occasionally I'd sing a major second or sixth against the triad, but I sensed that my efforts in that direction introduced very little edifying variety; the congregation's 'new song' (Psalm 33:3a) was quickly becoming old.

On one particular occasion a Christian friend of mine, concertmaster for the New York City Opera, brought his Guanerius violin to the service. At a lull in the worship he removed the masterfully made instrument from its case and played a Bach partita to the glory of God. It was a singularly enriching moment for me, something that is still fresh in my mind despite the passage of decades. He had offered up to Christ anew what, in the first instance, had also been offered to Him centuries before.

If you are at all musical, I want to encourage you to bring your song to God, even if it is—after Mendelssohn—a song without words. Play to Him, sing to Him—skilfully, if you can (Psalm 33:3b); offer your music up to Him when it seems you haven't got a prayer.

I gave my first public performance when I was five years old. People tell me I played well, although I can't imagine that my rendition of the *Warsaw Concerto* could have been all that extraordinary—after all, my tiny fingers couldn't even span an octave. Playing for the world was exciting, yet something far more satisfying marked my life.

Late in the afternoon my father would come home from a hard day's work, sit down on our living-room sofa, and ask me to play for him. He loved to hear me play. Perhaps it was my version of a ballad by Cole Porter or a jazzy number by Louis Armstrong. Whatever it was, my dad would sit there as if he was listening to Arthur Rubenstein or Vladimir Horowitz. Always appreciative of whatever my small fingers and limited skill could produce, his responsiveness made me want to play for him. And for years I did just that.

When I came to know Jesus Christ as my personal Lord and Friend, I also came to know Him as a Person who lovingly and appreciatively receives all that He enables me to bring Him. Jack Benny used to say that he cherished one friend in particular because, as long as he had known him, 'he never walked out on me when I played my violin'. There is a sense in which our Lord is like Jack's friend: He never walks out on us when we offer Him our song, our art—whatever we have.

I'm not suggesting that we employ some form of art as a substitute for prayer; perish the thought! Yet since the Bible makes it clear that worship is nothing less than the offering of ourselves up to God (Romans 12:1), is it not logical that art—one of His choicest gifts—can be a meaningful vehicle of worship, a valid complement to the words we bring to Him? And is it not your privilege, mandated by Scripture, to 'Sing and make music in your heart to the Lord' (Ephesians 5:19b)? Music is special: it was present at creation when the stars sang together (Job 38:7); God, Himself, sings (Zephaniah 3:17; see Matthew 26:30).

CRITICAL, YET RECEPTIVE

I don't suppose the name of Gilbert Kaplan means anything to most folk. Although Gilbert was not trained as a musician—he became a successful financier—as a boy he fell in love with Mahler's tremendously complex *Resurrection Symphony* and became so enthralled by the great work that, at age forty, he decided to find a way to conduct the immense score (the only kind Mahler seemed to compose).

Kaplan hired a live-in conductor and worked up to nine hours a day covering all the basics of conducting, then travelling to concert halls all over the world where the ninety-minute work was being performed. Marshalling his financial resources, he hired the American Symphony Orchestra for no less than twelve full rehearsals with chorus and vocal soloists. Finally, he rented New York's Avery Fisher Hall and, with three hundred and nineteen paid musicians, conducted the score from memory— Gilbert could not read music.

The result was astounding: the critics loved it and Kaplan's subsequent 1988 recording with the London Symphony Orchestra has been a best seller in the world of classics. Moreover, the successful conductor—with a repertory of one— has led many of the world's outstanding orchestras in one of Mahler's finest works.

Yet for all of that, there's no evidence that maestro Kaplan has pursued his musical venture out of love for God; the music does not appear to be an expression of his heart's desire to worship the Messiah. His audience is the world and that's the source of the appreciation he receives.

In a time and place remote from Mr. Kaplan's, 'All the Levites who were musicians—Asaph, Heman, Jeduthun and their sons and relatives—stood on the east side of the altar, dressed in fine linen and playing cymbals, harps, and lyres' (2 Chronicles 5:12). The Chronicler goes on to tell us that they were accompanied by 120 priests sounding trumpets (wouldn't even inventive Berlioz have been envious?)! 'Accompanied by trumpets, cymbals, and other instruments, they raised their voices in praise to the Lord and sang: "He is good; His love endures forever" (v.13).'

It's as refreshing today as it was then to see worshippers who are concerned that their offering is not only personally satisfying but, more to the point, meaningful to God. Once, in the days of Jehoshaphat, when the people of God were faced with military conflict, the choir led in the attack as they sang of God's *chesed,* His undeserved, faithful covenant-love (2 Chronicles 20:21). They knew that they were no better than their enemies over whom God had promised to make them victorious. Such recognition must also move us to worship Him and sing of His mercies (Lamentations 3:22-23).

God is not unimaginative when it comes to devising creative ways for His people to worship Him. Neither is He disinterested in the humble songs of two beaten men who raise their voices to Him at midnight (Acts 16:25). The question I must ask myself is this: For whom do I sing and play (or paint, write, compose)? If it is not directed out of love for my unseen audience—my Creator-Redeemer—all of my efforts ultimately become 'a resounding gong or a clanging cymbal' (1 Corinthians 13:1). But if, through the eyes of faith, I discern His presence and the fact that my skills are to be used for Him (1 Chronicles 25:7), all that I offer up to Him will be received with an appreciative graciousness far surpassing that of an earthly father's who simply loved to hear his little boy play the piano.

> *Let every creature rise and bring*
> *peculiar honours to our King;*
> *angels descend with songs again,*
> *and earth repeat the loud amen!*

Isaac Watts

12
Wrestling with God

However much we may find his behaviour offensive, the Bible sets forth Jacob as essentially a man of faith; he has a deep, abiding belief in God's promises—a conviction he holds unwaveringly. Unfortunately, Jacob also believes that those promises can only come to him through his own manipulativeness; thus, he is rightly called 'Jacob' or, if you'll allow a modern colloquialism in place of the accepted translation 'supplanter', we might call him 'clever dealer' (Genesis 27:36).

We all have the Jacob-like tendency to try to accomplish God's will in our own strength and cleverness. This is particularly true when, like Jacob, we have to deal with obstinate people or hostile situations. It's easy to commiserate with a man whose father seemed altogether oblivious to God's purposes (Genesis 25:23) and whose militant brother was 'godless' (Hebrews 12:16). Add a doting, enterprising mother and you've created quite an unhealthy spiritual climate. It was in such an environment that Jacob determined to do everything necessary—fair or foul—to achieve what he believed was coming to him.

BUSINESS AS USUAL

There is a problem when we pursue objectives—even noble ones—with Jacob's orientation: our own efforts take centre-stage and our conscious reliance on God diminishes. We may soon come to the place where we find prayer to be unimportant, engaging in it somewhat perfunctorily. Eventually God compassionately engineers our lives to make us aware of the fruitlessness of this approach to life; by His grace He helps us see that our problems cannot be satisfactorily resolved with Him on the sidelines.

Coming to that realization may necessitate painful experiences; Jacob knew that to be so. For about twenty years, Jacob was allowed to follow his self-styled pathway to the desired blessings. But the consequences of the patriarch's deceitful ways drove him from his home and an embittered brother to the home of his uncle Laban, no stranger himself to dealing with others in a self-serving manner. There Jacob wound up on the receiving end of a manipulative relative and, perhaps expectantly, responded in kind. Once again, Jacob was forced to turn tail and run—this time with Laban and company in angry pursuit.

A DECISIVE OPPORTUNITY

Before ever arriving at Laban's camp, however, God appeared to Jacob in a dream. As he slept under the open sky he saw a ladder upon which angels were journeying to and from heaven. One remarkable aspect of the vision is the fact that God did not speak a word of rebuke to the wily refugee; rather, He came to Him enlarging upon those precious promises which Jacob had found to be so elusive (Genesis 28:13-15).

Although Jacob had little time for spiritual things, God had plenty of time for Jacob. There in the desert God took the initiative—'He found him at Bethel' (Hosea 12:4)—to remind Jacob that the blessings He sought could only be his through grace.

Jacob's consequent vow to give God a tenth of all he would acquire may have been well motivated, but it was entirely superfluous. Whatever Jacob could do, no ladder of human origin could link his earthly need with heaven's provisions; only the Son of God—upon whom even the angels focus (John 1:51)—could transform the place of Jacob's exile to a 'Bethel', where, as the name implies, the presence of God might be known. Perhaps, like Jacob, you're in what seems to you to be a nondescript place of exile—I know the feeling! In your discouragement you may feel that you haven't a prayer. Nothing could be further from the truth. Our Lord can transform your Luz into Bethel (Genesis 28:19).

THE DARKNESS DEEPENS

As Jacob neared Esau's country he sent a message informing Esau of his imminent arrival. The returning news made Jacob fear that Esau, with hundreds of men, was coming to avenge himself against Jacob for his earlier crafty dealings concerning the birthright. Jacob was undone! There he stood, all alone at the river Jabbok (Genesis 32:24).

There in his isolation he not only came face-to-face with his weakness but also with God who appeared as an angelic being. Moses tells us that a wrestling match ensued and that, in the process, the angel 'touched' Jacob's hip, throwing it out of joint (32:25). Some folk have tended to identify Jacob as the hero in this encounter. While we may find Jacob's perseverance praiseworthy we dare not lose sight of other key factors revealed in the account.

First, it is quite clear that God took the initiative to wrestle with

Jacob (Genesis 32:24); second, God imposed limits upon Himself so as to not destroy Jacob; and finally, God did so in order to enable Jacob to understand that God was striving to bring His blessings to His unworthy, but deeply loved, child. It was out of desperation that Jacob 'wept and begged for the Angel's favour' (Hosea 12:4). For all of his previous cleverness, Jacob had only succeeded in alienating people; and he himself had become little more than a hapless vagabond.

Jacob's encounters with God at Bethel and Peniel made him face the hopelessness of his plight apart from the grace of God. Not only had he come face-to-face with God but also with the foolishness of trying to prosper by his own wits. The change of his name to 'Israel' (God strives) served to remind Jacob of God's gracious intentions, as did his perpetual limp, the result of God's touch (about which we will yet have more to say). How sad to realise that my people's remembrance of Jacob's life-changing experience lives on primarily as an adjunct to their dietary code (Genesis 32:32).

A RABBINICAL LESSON

As I was preparing to become a son of the commandment ('bar mitzvah'), the rabbi met me in his study. We spoke about the religious matters I had to pursue in order to become a man in the sight of Israel and embrace fully the yoke of the law. As we spoke, the rabbi's throat became dry and he arose from his desk, crossing the book-lined room to his newly acquired drinking machine, one which would give him boiling water for tea or iced water, should he desire it. A look of disgust came over him as he stared at his cup's contents; it was tepid—undrinkable. That his unpleasant experience might not be a total loss, he turned to me and, in true rabbinical fashion, drew an object lesson from his disappointment, saying,

'Stuart, let this serve to teach you never to involve yourself with anything that runs both hot and cold.'

A BIBLICAL PARALLEL
The New Testament teaches us that God also despises lukewarmness, especially in spiritual matters (Revelation 3:16). How fortunate for us that God strives with us to free us from the doldrums of a lacklustre relationship with Him; He loves us too much to allow us to simply subsist on the husks of our own religious efforts.

As it was with Jacob, so it is with us: God engineers our lives so that we'll ultimately cast off all self-reliance and trust solely in His mighty power. All of our calamities have been sovereignly designed to cause us to develop a fervency which drives us to Christ humbly and dependently—even desperately. Through Jacob's painful humbling the patriarch personally learned the meaning of the word, 'trust'. It was by way of his limp that he had been made whole.

The Hebrew word for 'trust' finds its root in the idea of being cast prostrate upon a supporting object. Isaiah 26:3 tells us that God brings perfect peace to the one who trusts in—is cast upon—the Lord. Whatever is happening in your life be assured of this: God will take away every prop in your life until you find your sufficiency in Jesus. He wrestles with us until we're truly convinced that He alone is our Sustainer, not only in life's calamities when we may feel we have nowhere else to turn but also in the context of those mundane daily situations which we foolishly believe we can handle by ourselves.

I'm told 'God helps those who help themselves'. Yet the Bible never puts much stock in man's ability to provide for himself. That's why God wants me to come to Him in a spirit of self-distrust and submissiveness, trusting Him to keep His own promises in His own way. That way is always good for it invariably leads me to my Saviour. Author-speaker Stephen Brown was right when he said, 'Sometimes you don't know Jesus is all you need until Jesus is all you've got.'

> Though like the wanderer,
> The sun gone down,
> Darkness be over me,
> My rest a stone;
> Yet in my dreams I'd be
> Nearer, my God, to Thee,
> Nearer to Thee.
>
> There let the way appear
> Steps unto heaven;
> All that Thou sendest me
> In mercy given;
> Angels to beckon me
> Nearer, my God, to Thee,
> Nearer to Thee.
>
> Then, with my waking thoughts
> Bright with Thy praise,
> Out of my stony griefs
> Bethel I'll raise;
> So by my woes to be
> Nearer, my God, to Thee,
> Nearer to Thee.   Sarah Adams, 1841

In the final analysis, *When You Haven't Got a Prayer* is not only grammatically incorrect, it flies in the face of one of Jesus' most precious promises: 'All that the Father gives Me will come to Me, and whoever comes to Me I will never drive away' (John

6:37). Although I run hot and cold, God's love for me never waxes or wanes. He's always ready to receive me, like the father of Jesus' well-known parable who embraces his returning son, falls upon the filthy swineherd's neck and kisses him passionately (Luke 15:20).

Like the lost sheep, my main contribution to my spiritual well-being consists in His finding me and bringing me home (Luke 15:5-6). Even when I believe I'm full of spiritual zeal, my life's foundational prayer is for His restorative grace (Psalm 119:176). And He whose shoulders bear the weight of governments (Isaiah 9:6) also gladly bears my weight—even as He did His cross.

13
The Glory of the Ordinary

I indicated at the outset that prayer is not easy for me; in fact, praying is something I really struggle to do. I've read about folk who have achieved what appear to be marvellous victories in their prayer lives. I recall J. Sidlow Baxter telling of his own progress as a young pastor, how he experienced a breakthrough in prayer by not giving into his emotional reluctance to pray, taking those emotions in tow as he disciplined himself to persevere in his devotional life.

His experience, while apparently gloriously valid for him, has not found much of a parallel in my life. If there's anything I find tremendously difficult, it's praying for more than fifteen minutes at a time, especially if I'm in a fixed position. Like my ancient forbears I like to stand praying, even pacing a bit in the process.

But when I read about my Lord Jesus spending many hours of uninterrupted communion with His Father I yearn for something of greater substance. I would love to be transported to realms of glory, to be 'caught up to paradise' (2 Corinthians 12:4). As I read Paul's cryptic account of his vision I envy him. How that experience must have inspired him to pray, to worship, to rejoice.

Yet as precious as prayer is, there's something of greater worth to consider: your preciousness to Jesus Christ. You need to see yourself the way God sees you. That's the only way to deal with prayerlessness, not to mention life's anxieties and fears.

A CASE IN POINT

The young Hebrew, Gideon, was in hiding because of his enemies, the Midianites, when God appeared to him with words of comfort and hope (Judges 6:12). At first the fearful man recoiled from receiving God's words; Gideon thought himself totally inadequate to be the means for his own deliverance, let alone his people's (Judges 6:15). It was not until 'The Spirit of the Lord put on Gideon' (6:34) that Gideon realised not only his full potential but, more essentially, his full worth to God. God delighted to relate to a simple, ordinary human in need and, through His transforming grace, saw Gideon as mighty (6:12).

This event typifies our situation. We don't naturally seek God's help; we're like this 'mighty man of valour',—what delightful humour—in retreat, hiding, until the Almighty seeks us out, reaches down to lift us up, and establishes us solidly on Christ.

Having lived in New York City, I often passed by the RCA building on Fifth Avenue. As one draws near the entrance he cannot fail to be impressed by the prominent sculpture of Atlas, struggling as he bears the weight of the world on his shoulders. There are multitudes who are living embodiments of that sorry figure, bending—as the Christmas carol tells it—'beneath life's crushing load'.

Many have become so used to relating to life in that posture that they have long ceased to look for a viable alternative. Right across the street is Saint Patrick's Cathedral. Behind its high altar one may find a sculpture of Jesus, presented as an unassuming lad, effortlessly holding up the world in one hand.

For nearly half of my life I lived—existed—as one beneath the crushing load of life; but my Messiah has called me to something far different, far better. He who has effortless control of all things also bears my weight as I entrust myself to Him.

CODA and REPRISE

We need to be constantly reminded of the fact that there is no intrinsic merit to our prayers, that God receives us without any reference to any of our efforts to behave spiritually. Recognizing daily how much He loves you not only transforms your view of life, it also changes your view of prayer. For so many, prayer is little more than a duty; when it is neglected, feelings of guilt and self-deprecation often plague their consciences.

The only cure for these negative experiences is a massive dose of grace. Grace is the most precious word in our vocabulary. My irregular prayer life can no more block out His unconditional love for me than a flyspeck can shut out the sun. Grace is the foundation for absolutely everything. It is because of grace that we're able to call God our Father; it is because of grace that we're able to seek Him, to serve Him, to love Him.

A friend of mine used to travel with Toscanini and the NBC Symphony in order to photograph the maestro, a musical genius whose behaviour was anything but conventional. Once the renowned conductor was trying to help bass-baritone Robert Merrill sing a syncopated musical phrase which was causing the Metropolitan Opera soloist some difficulty. As an instructor, Toscanini was anything but patient—especially with other professionals. He bent over from the podium and began tapping the rhythm on the singer's head until the singer had mastered the music. For years afterwards

Merrill could never sing that composition without feeling the presence of an invisible baton on his head.

Whenever you and I speak about prayer or service or devotion to Christ we need to feel the presence of our heavenly Maestro (Master) tapping, as it were, the sublime rhythm of the phrase 'by grace alone' upon the very fibre of our beings. Say it aloud. Say it again and again. Sing it to the three 'G's' and one 'E-flat' of Beethoven's opening measures to his brilliant *Fifth Symphony*: BY GRACE A-LONE! ... BY GRACE ALONE! There are no syncopated difficulties to overcome here; only the reluctance of our wayward hearts to receive the truth of which He is both Composer and Performer.

When we are fully persuaded that He is truly the God of grace, prayer rightly becomes simply and solely our response to His undeserved favour. With that perspective we see prayer not as a burden or even a responsibility; it is our soul's logical response to so great an unmerited love. The vantage point of grace convinces us that He really is concerned with everything that touches our lives; and the love of Christ compels us to worship Him—to come to Him as an empty-handed little child in anticipation of an altogether gracious reception.

The Father of whom Jesus spoke in Luke 15 is truly prodigal; His lavishness far exceeds that of His wastrel son. See! How He gazes down the road, longing for the fellowship of the one whose empty stomach would, at great length, give rise to his words of repentance. Look! How the Father makes a public spectacle of Himself, running down the road to embrace His filthy son, interrupting the boy's carefully framed confession and kissing him again and again. Behold! How the Patriarch bestows His divine dignity and wealth upon the one who was so terribly lost.

'How great is the love the Father has lavished on us, that we should be called children of God' (1 John 3:1). The words, 'how great', in the original mean 'from what country'; they convey the awesome amazement that the apostle experienced as he contemplated God's love personally entering the world from its distant origin. Why should He humiliate Himself and endure the cross? *Why?* When you've answered that question you are not only ready to pray, you are unable to refrain from doing so. For the answer makes it clear that His love is not induced by anything that is intrinsically ours.

In the days of Moses the people were told that their blessedness was in no way related to their qualities but, rather, because of the love that God had for them (Deuteronomy 7:7-8). Many generations would pass until the time when that principle found its full expression on a stinking hill outside Jerusalem. No one sums up that principle better than that former Pharisee, liberated by grace, when he wrote: 'But God demonstrates His own love for us in this: While we were still sinners, Christ died for us' (Romans 5:8).

WHOLENESS THROUGH BROKENNESS

Many years ago I had the privilege of conducting Jerome Hine's opera on the life of Christ in which Mr. Hines sang the title role. The splendid production offered up Biblical vignettes from the life of Christ, culminating with the Lord's Supper. With vivid realism the audience beheld a simply robed, towering figure breaking bread, giving it to his disciples, and singing of his abiding presence for them and all following generations.

From my vantage point one could observe something very special: many of the disciples were weeping; they had been touched by the reality which often eludes us but which Isaiah distantly foresaw when He prophesied, 'Surely He took up our sicknesses and carried our sorrows ... He was crushed on account of our iniquities; the punishment by which our peace is affected was upon Him; and by His wounds healing has come to us' (53:4-5, author's transl.)

The singer-actors in Hine's musical drama were Christians (except, ironically, for the chap playing Judas Iscariot who was, unlike his biblical counterpart, converted following the drama); on stage the invisible realm had become real to them as they pondered anew what God had done for them. The transformed cast found it difficult to weep and sing, yet they managed to do so.

In our sorrows we also find it difficult to sing, to praise, to pray. How can we utter Zion's songs in this benighted place? Yet by the power of the Spirit we recall that God actually walked among us and allowed Himself for our sakes to be broken and crushed. This same God promised never to leave us or forsake us (Hebrews 13:5). So, as the poet said, 'Earth's crammed with heaven, and every common bush afire with God.' If we were to truly glimpse reality each of us would see himself as the common bush in whom God would glow more brightly.

We cleave to the message of Easter morn yet we live in a Good Friday world. But it will not always be so. Our Father has placed His inextinguishable hope in our hearts. It not only makes a good breakfast but also—contrary to the old aphorism—a palatable dinner. If your hope and my hope were an error, we would concur with Chesterton that 'the error could hardly have lasted a day. If it were mere ecstasy, it would seem that such an ecstasy could not endure for an hour.'

But our hope has endured for two thousand years. That hope must ultimately thrive because the God of hope 'has poured out His love into our hearts by the Holy Spirit, whom He has given us' (Romans 5:5). He has invaded our ordinary sphere to quicken our hope in the midst of frustration; and He gives us patience to wait for His glorious deliverance (Romans 8:20-25), even giving us a prayer when we think we cannot pray (Romans 8:26-27). Everything in God's Word is designed to give us hope (Romans 15:4), to encourage us to pray even when the odds seem overwhelmingly against us.

When my life seemed it was falling apart, a dear friend and fellow elder repeatedly said, 'The best is yet to come.'

The only way to accept that and find sustenance in it is by looking to Him who will give us His joy and peace as we trust in Him (Romans 15:13); and He who never gives grudgingly will, according to the apostle, cause us to 'overflow with hope'. When we are unable to soar on wings like eagles—mountain top experiences are few and far between—we are told He vindicates our hope in Him by giving us grace to 'walk and not be faint' (Isaiah 40:31). There, especially, the ordinary becomes glorious.

14

The Problem of Joy

'I have told you this so that my joy may be in you and that your joy may be complete' (John 15:11).
'I say these things while an still in the world so that they may have the full measure of my joy within them' (John 17:13)

There are no less than ten words for joy (or rejoicing) in the Hebrew Old Testament. No other tongue rivals the Hebrew language in its diversity and comprehensiveness on this subject. But the abundant Scriptural references to joy - the Psalms leading all the books - only tend to draw attention to the lack of it in most of our lives.

Is joy a problem for you? Would you characterise your life as being essentially joyful? Perhaps joy seems as elusive as the will-o'-the-wisp. It is clear from John's texts that Jesus wants His disciples to experience joy. It is His gift to us; it is Jesus' joy. But what is its nature and how do you get it?

It strikes me as remarkable that Jesus spoke of His joy on the night of His betrayal by Judas, on the evening before He embraced His cross. One might have expected the Lord to be thoroughly pensive and solemn irrespective of the celebratory nature of the Passover.

There is a question asked in the Talmud why Yahweh appointed so many feasts for Israel. The Rabbis answered that it was because God wanted His people to be joyous. In Jewish circles, perhaps the best known word for joy, *simcha*, is often linked to God's commandments; *Simchat Torah* is the festival of rejoicing over the Law. Annually, especially among the orthodox, this is an occasion to commemorate the distinct privilege which is uniquely Israel's: they were the recipients of the Almighty's holy will. The celebrants - along with ancient Judah's sweet singer - revel in the joy that His precepts give them (Psalm 19:8). Observing the enthusiasm of worship of the *Hasidim* (most fervent of the Hebrews) one might think them to be 'Semitic Pentecostals'. Their rabbis teach that, when the Messiah comes, He will enforce the perfect keeping of the Law as an integral part of establishing the kingdom of God.

I have never been able to rejoice in the Torah. I can speak of its flawlessness but must in the same breath acknowledge my own imperfection. The Law hovers above me as a shroud, revealing this dead man's corruption. I cannot delight in it any more that I can rejoice in an instrument of death. But I do receive it as the revelation of God's perfect moral character and rejoice in the fact that my righteous Messiah has fulfilled it perfectly on my behalf - that, as Jesus said to His Father, 'I have brought You glory on earth by completing the work You gave Me to do' (John 17:4). He is *Yahweh Tzidkenu*, the Lord our righteousness (Jeremiah 23:6).

Simcha also occurs in another context which speaks with compelling clarity of a fullness of joy derived not from contemplating the commandments but, rather, from anticipating the future: You have made known to me the path of life; You will fill me with joy (plural in the Heb.) in Your presence, with eternal pleasures at Your right hand (Psalm 16:11).

Frequent readers of the New Testament will recall that this great verse plays a central part in the very first apostolic message preached to the people of Israel (Acts 2:28). And the joy of Peter's witness, like that of David's, was bound up with the fact of the Holy One's - the Messiah's - resurrection (Psalm 16:10).

There is an utterly depressing joylessness which grips the heart of one who feels he's been abandoned. I recall a frightful dream when I was young. I dreamed I had been thrown into a pit, along with other prisoners of a Nazi death camp. As I lay helpless I looked up to see an executioner about to pour lye upon me and my comrades. I could see the toxic substance coming closer and closer, about to eat into my flesh. A sense of abandonment - of being altogether alone - paralysed me with dread. How unlike the Psalmist who testifies to his joyful security in God: "My flesh shall rest in safety ... You will not abandon me to the pit..." (16:10)

This was also at the heart of Jesus' joy. The night of sorrow was at hand. Yet the day of triumph was not far away. There was a joy filling Jesus' consciousness which enabled Him to endure the cross, scorning its shame (Hebrews 12:2). He knew that His suffering would not endure but that His joy would! Victory's pervasive power moulded His thoughts even on the night of imminent anguish: "Now is the Son of Man glorified" (John 13:31) revealed a preoccupation with the blessed outcome of His passion.

Jesus wants us to know the kind of joy He knew - joy which survives - even thrives - in life's deepest pits.

Our Saviour tells us that a time is coming when no one will

take away our joy (John 16:22). In that day we will hear Him say, "enter into the joy of your Master" (Matthew 25:21, 23). Yet joy's eschatological dimension must also invade our lives today: Jesus is concerned with our current needs: ... I say these things while I am still in the world so that they may have the full measure of My joy within them (John 17:13).

What did Jesus' disciples hear Him say which would have given them joy? Much able biblical exposition has been written to broaden the reader's understanding of the enriching truths of Jesus' longest prayer. After all is said, however, joy springs from the recurrent thought that God loves me and that Christ, Himself, has become inextricably joined to my life (John 15:9, 16:27; 17:26). It is an amazing truth that, according to Jesus' teaching, God the Father actually loves me as intensely as He loves His begotten Son.

The final moments of the Passover observance were filled with singing. The Hallel Psalms (113-118) were probably the last songs Jesus sang with His disciples before His death. Prominent in the last of these Psalms is a witness to both the rejection and exaltation of the Messiah: The stone the builders rejected has become the cornerstone ... (118:22).

As the Christ and His tiny flock sang these words, only the Master understood the text's prophetic poignancy. Sorrowful, yet rejoicing, He knew that His soul's travail would forge the way to a more glorious dawn than the world had ever seen. Undergirded by that truth He took the dark path to Gethsemane and Golgotha. His most articulate spokesman knew the resultant power of that route: ... dying, and yet we live on; beaten, and yet not killed; sorrowful, yet always rejoicing; poor, yet making many rich; having nothing, and yet possessing everything (2 Corinthians 6:9-10).

A Muslim inquirer asked me how it was ethically possible for God to allow the righteous *Isa* (Jesus) to suffer. The answer, in part, must be found in the Divine design to bring His people joy. Divine economics teaches that only He who was without sin could pay the redemptive price of another's sin; and, having done so, He assures us that He has established a future for us that is more wonderful than we could ever imagine (1 Corinthians 2:9).

There is an ancient Jewish aphorism which states, "All Israel has a share in the world to come." But there is no statement which remotely approaches the magnitude of the promise "that when He appears we shall be like Him, for we shall see Him as He is" (1 John 3:2).

For the child of God no suffering is ever ultimate. The valley of tears may be the place of our bivouac but it is not our permanent encampment. Perhaps it's possible to be so heavenly minded that we're of no earthly good but I have yet to meet anyone whose thoughts of heaven diminished his worth on earth. A disciplined focus is the surest route to joy if the crux is right. For Jesus, the joy which lay ahead made the present griefs tolerable, even bitter-sweet.

Christ's victory lay in the breaking of the power of evil and nullifying the power of death. His death's intent was to free multitudes from their enslavement to these otherwise unconquerable forces. Ours is a vicarious victory - vicarious, yet also shared because, through simple trust, we recognise our lives to be mysteriously (though effectively) bound up with His (2 Corinthians 1:21).

There was a time in the Hebrew's people's Babylonian captivity when their captors "demanded songs of joy; they said, 'Sing us one of the songs of Zion!' " (Psalm 137:3). But emotions cannot be commanded. "How," said the Jews, "can we sing the songs of the Lord in a foreign land" (137:4)? Their hearts were downcast for they were faraway from Jerusalem, their highest joy (verse 6). Many centuries later another exile, the disciple John, was instructed to record his vision for our encouragement:

> I saw the Holy City, the new Jerusalem, coming down out of heaven from God, prepared as a bride beautifully dressed for her husband. And I heard a loud voice from the throne saying, 'Now the dwelling of God is with men, and He will live with them. They will be His people, and God Himself will be with them and be their God. He will wipe every tear from their eyes. There will be no more death or mourning or crying or pain, for the old order of things has passed away'.

"Therefore," prayed A W Tozer, "whatever of Thyself Thou hast been pleased to disclose, help me to search out as treasure more precious than rubies or the merchandise of fine gold; for with Thee shall I live when the stars of the twilight are no more and the heavens have vanished away and only Thou remainest."

According to the Talmud, there is no *simcha* without wine. Yet sometime "there are no grapes on the wines ..." (Habakkuk 3:17). Joy in distressful situations is only possible as a fruit of the Holy Spirit (Galatians 5:22). And it is only through the Spirit's movement in our hearts that we may experience a joy that sustains us in our adversities. Therefore one of the simplest and most meaningful prayers me by: "Lord, may Your Holy Spirit make Your promises real to me." We have every reason to hope that He will for, as Jesus said, "If you, though you are evil, know how to give good gifts to your children, how much more will your Father in heaven give the Holy Spirit to those who ask Him" (Luke 11:13)? He whose faithfulness is beyond reproach will not long leave us comfortless (John 14:18).

> O Joy that seekest me through pain,
> I cannot close my heart to Thee;
> I trace the rainbow through the rain,
> And feel the promise is not vain
> That morn shall tearless be.
>
> George Matheson

An Historical Postscript
15
"The God of the Eleventh Hour"

When things get bad, we may apply a most helpful salve by remembering God's gracious acts in history. This is how Asaph was refreshed as he was besieged by anxious thoughts (Psalm 77:7-12). Other psalms, too, invite the reader to consider God's historical actions in order to find encouragement (78, 105, 106). In addition, we need to relive some of our own past events to find peace and joy in troubled times.

My wife and I were newly married, living in a small Brooklyn apartment, a bit disoriented as we wondered what God had in mind for us. A gifted Metropolitan Opera baritone, Calvin Marsh, had suggested the possibility of my becoming his pianist-arranger, giving concerts together and using them as the means of sharing our testimonies to His grace. It was to be a faith-ministry: we'd receive free-will offerings at our concerts and simply trust God to provide for our needs. Our repertoire would be diverse, thereby ministering to a variety of tastes—to the end, that we might win people for Christ.

Developing such a musical program would involve much

planning and practice; therein lay a perplexing problem: I didn't own a piano. How could we possibly proceed without one? Lacking the necessary finances, I tried to get a loan. However, our local bank—whose commercials assured me that I had a friend there—wouldn't give me the time of day. According to their financial officer, the worst risks for loan repayments were musicians and ministers; I was both! I couldn't even borrow enough to buy a used instrument.

Sharon and I prayed for God's help; more specifically, that if He wanted us to launch out on a musical ministry He would help us get a piano. We had to make our decision soon if we were to plan an itinerary for the fall, so we asked Him to provide the instrument by a certain date, several weeks away. Yet we had exhausted all our resources. A close Jewish relative had offered me a Steinway Grand but only if I'd play it without reference to Jesus.

It was then that we received an unexpected visit from a Christian woman who had been teaching school in Connecticut. Gail was as poor as a proverbial churchmouse but was spiritually vital; she truly loved her Saviour. We all read the Word together and prayed together; she was a delightful friend to have visit, particularly at a time when we sensed we needed all the prayer support we could get.

Late one evening, Gail made an incredible announcement: 'The Lord wants me to get you a piano, a new one—the piano of your choice.' I was shocked and may have, following an ancient precedent, even laughed incredulously (Genesis 18:12). Where would she come up with the money for that kind of acquisition? She was not put off by my unbelief and proceeded to tell us that God had clearly indicated to her that this was His will in the matter; there was no point in debating it further. Gail was so convinced, in fact, that she zealously pooled virtually all of her material resources in order to help bring God's intentions to fruition.

To Whom Be the Glory?

At first Sharon and I were dumbfounded but quickly got the message: God had heard our prayer and Gail was the means to His answer.

We called the Yamaha dealer and arranged for the delivery of a grand piano. The soonest he could get it to us would be the last day of the month, at the very termination of that period in which we had asked God to answer our prayer. The marvellous instrument arrived on the 31st—the final delivery of the day!

A quarter-century later that piano sits prominently in our home as a reminder of the fact that God often answers our prayers a minute before it would have been too late; and that He typically works in the most unlikely manner—often employing the strangest means—in response to our cries for help.

As an expression of gratitude, my wife told Gail that we'd put a plaque on the piano acknowledging her gift. She demured! It was *not* her idea; it was the Lord's. If we chose to give anyone the credit it would have to go to Him with whom 'we always have a prayer'.

BIBLIOGRAPHY

John Baillie, **A Diary of Private Prayer,** (Charles Scribner's Sons, 1949).

Arthur Bennett, **The Valley of Vision: A Collection of Puritan Prayers,** (Banner of Truth Trust, 1986).

Jerry Bridges, **Trusting God,** (Navpress, 1988).

Elisabeth Elliot, **These Strange Ashes,** (Harper and Row, 1985).

Soren Kierkegaard, selected prayers dating from 1847-1855 contained in Samuel Barber's choral-symphonic score, **Prayers of Kierkegaard,** (G. Schirmer, 1955).

C. S. Lewis, **Letters to Malcolm: Chiefly on Prayer,** (Harcourt, Brace and World, 1963).

John Newton, **The Works of John Newton,** (Banner of Truth Trust, 1985).

J. I. Packer, **Knowing God,** (InterVarsity Press, 1979).

Richard L. Pratt, Jr., **Pray With Your Eyes Open,** (Presbyterian and Reformed Publishing Co., 1987).

Derek Prime, **Created to Praise,** (Christian Focus Publications, 1993).

Wayne R. Spear, **The Theology of Prayer,** (Baker Book House, 1979).

Paul Tournier, **Reflections,** (Harper and Row, 1976).

John White, **Daring to Draw Near,** (InterVarsity Press, 1978).

```
┌─────────────────────────────┐
│         Books on            │
│         **Prayer**          │
│        published by         │
│  Christian Focus Publications│
└─────────────────────────────┘
```

The Prayer Life of Jesus
David M McIntyre

ISBN 1 85792 010 4 (pocket paperback) 160 PAGES

Prayer, one of the most difficult disciplines for the Christian. Jesus, the best role model for our whole life. Take these two and we have the ingredients for a fascinating and challenging book.

The Hidden Life of Prayer
David M McIntyre

ISBN 1871676 258 (pocket paperback) 128 PAGES

A book which stimulates our prayer life by looking at the examples of notable Christians from all periods of church history. The author, a former Principal of Glasgow Bible College, was the son-in-law of Andrew Bonar whose diary is a spiritual classic on the prayer-life.

Spurgeon's Prayers
ISBN 1 85792 0414 (B format) 160 PAGES
Twenty-six actual prayers of Spurgeon, together with a short address on the conduct of prayer meetings.

Practical Prayer
Derek Prime
ISBN 1 871 676 51 7 (pocket paperback) 128 PAGES
An ideal guidebook for young Christians. The Holy Spirit's help is explained and our thoughts are directed to the Person to whom we pray. The author was pastor of Charlotte Chapel, Edinburgh for several years but is now involved in worldwide conference speaking as well as in writing.

A Method For Prayer
Matthew Henry
ISBN 1 85792 068 6 (B Format) 288 PAGES
A systematic and biblical approach to prayer, written by the famous Bible commentator, which gives examples of prayers in the Bible, different types of prayer, and helpful hints on making the most of our communication with God. Included in this book is the author's well-known classic, *Directions For Daily Communion With God.*